HALF
A PIECE OF
CLOTH

HALF
A PIECE OF
CLOTH

*The courage of Africa's
countless widows*

JANE L CRANE

Introduction by Emily Onyango Ph D

Cover & book design: Chris Gander, United Kingdom.

Front and back cover photos of widows (except one noted below) by Grace Winsome Zinkievich © 2013.
Back cover photo of author with widow by International Justice Mission.
All interior photos by Jane L. Crane unless otherwise noted.

Published by Hearkening Press, PO Box 9105, Rancho Santa Fe, California, 92067, USA. Printed and bound in the United States of America, the United Kingdom, and Australia.

Hearkeningpress.com

DEDICATION

To Rebecca and the others who cared for me when I was a child in Georgia, leaving your children at home, because I was white and you were black, and you had no other choice.

CONTENTS

Ten Minutes That Changed My Life 1

Introduction by Emily Onyango, Ph.D. 2

ONE   Women as 'Property' 5

PART I – WIDOWS' STORIES 25

TWO   Under Rwanda's Spreading Uminyinya Tree 27

THREE   Threads of Hope in Ghana 53

FOUR   Valor in Uganda 75

FIVE   Honor in a South African Township 101

SIX   Riches in the Congo 125

SEVEN   Breakthrough in Zambia 149

PART II – SOLUTIONS 171

EIGHT   Two of Africa's Finest 173

NINE   Religion: Helping or Hurting? 191

TEN   A Whole Piece of Cloth 213

Notes 233

Bibliography 249

Acknowledgements 255

About the Author 257

TEN MINUTES THAT CHANGED MY LIFE

At last I was at the United Nations. For years I'd wanted to go to its annual conference on women. Now I was one of 4,000 delegates, wandering the crowded halls, trying to decide which of many workshops to attend. The year was 2007.

I located an auditorium hosting what I hoped would be an interesting panel discussion, ideally about women's land issues in Africa. I'd become intrigued by that and wanted to know more.

Only one speaker stood out to me: Elizabeth Mataka, born in Botswana, living in Zambia, a Global Ambassador to Africa for the UN. At the end of her eloquent ten-minute talk, my life had changed. She said many widows in Sub-Saharan Africa are blamed for their husbands' deaths because of superstition and cast out of their homes by the husbands' relatives, sometimes without their children. With the wildfire of HIV/AIDS, she said, the number of poor widows suffering such a fate had escalated dramatically.

In a way I didn't fully understand, my life became intertwined that day with the lives of these widows. I was working on a Master's degree in Peace and Justice then, and I decided to write my thesis on women's land issues in Sub-Saharan Africa, including how widows suffer. After that, I wanted to hear from the widows themselves. My African women friends encouraged me, a white western woman, to follow this pursuit and tell the stories internationally.

So many widows came forth that I interviewed more than 60 in seven African countries over three years. Here are their stories, and mine, as I traveled into their homes and lives to share these stories with you. May their courage inspire you as much as it has me.

Jane L. Crane

INTRODUCTION

The cry of Africa's widows rises across our continent. As continents go, we have more than our share due to HIV/AIDS, wars and conflict, and the indignities of widespread poverty. Yet their voices have largely been neglected and deserve to be heard. In this book, Jane Crane gives many that chance.

She tackles the widows' stories in seven countries, setting the scene first with interesting background about each one. Then readers hear from the women themselves. This is in tune with the African way of telling stories and gives the widows voice to share their own stories of oppression and how they have dealt with the issues at hand. The style of the book is excellent and refreshing to read. After I began it, I found it hard to put down.

When we talk of the plight of widows across Africa, this is not just a generalization but what happens in reality. If you analyze the word *widow* used by most groups, it usually means "wife of the grave," implying that even at death the man still owns the woman. Traditionally, a woman is not married to an individual but to the family, so when the husband dies she is still property of that family.

Many people want to attribute certain practices to traditional culture, however, closer study reveals these to be later inventions for exploitation and oppression. They are used to torment and humiliate widows, who then become vulnerable.

In many cases, men are the oppressors. But it may be the husband's sisters and other female members of his family who become the worst tormentors of the widow, all in the name of culture.

Property rights for widows are now enshrined in the constitution of many African countries, but they are not guaranteed unless women have the knowledge and courage to stand up for them.

Even educated women may be denied access to some of the property from the marriage after the husband's death and be intimidated to participate in oppressive rituals.

The stories in this book capture the oppression and exploitation of widows but also their courage and hope. As they tell their stories to the author, they experience healing. The widows who read this book will also find healing. Other readers will be challenged to participate in widows' empowerment and justice.

The author also shows how the stories of some of the widows offer solutions for others to learn from. These widows are not just showing desperation, but they have the solutions within them. Giving the widows voice to tell these solutions in their own words is empowering for them and for others.

The brief fictional stories at the end of each chapter make for good reading and employ a powerful method of communication in Africa. This form is a good way of weaving culture with other issues like injustice and justice, oppression and empowerment, poverty, and gender-based violence.

The line that cuts across the book is education as a major tool of empowerment. If educated, widows can make decisions about their lives, be empowered economically, and be independent. Then they can come up with their own solutions to their problems. They can also influence other widows toward better lives.

Lastly, religion is central in Africa, as Jane discusses in this book, and Christianity is predominant in Sub-Saharan Africa. So the Church is in a strategic place to influence culture and world view on this important subject. It is time for the Church in Africa to arise from its slumber and speak out on behalf of its countless widows.

Emily Onyango, Ph.D.
Dean of Students, St. Paul's University, Limuru, Kenya

WESTERN SAHARA
MOROCCO
TUNISIA
ALGERIA
LIBYA
EGYPT
MAURITANIA
MALI
NIGER
SENEGAL
GAMBIA
GUINEA BISSAU
GUINEA
SIERRA LEONE
LIBERIA
BURKINA FASO
COTE D'IVOIRE
GHANA
TOGO
BENIN
NIGERIA
CHAD
SUDAN
ERITREA
DJIBOUTI
CENTRAL AFRICAN REPUBLIC
SOUTH SUDAN
ETHIOPIA
SOMALIA
CAMEROON
EQUATORIAL GUINEA
GABON
CONGO REPUBLIC
CABINDA
DEMOCRATIC REPUBLIC OF THE CONGO
UGANDA
RWANDA
BURUNDI
KENYA
TANZANIA
ANGOLA
ZAMBIA
MALAWI
COMOROS
MOZAMBIQUE
MADAGASCAR
NAMIBIA
ZIMBABWE
BOTSWANA
SWAZILAND
LESOTHO
SOUTH AFRICA

NORTH AFRICA
SUB-SAHARAN AFRICA

1

WOMEN AS 'PROPERTY'

"The god that owns a woman is the husband that married her."

African saying[1]

An African friend became a well-educated professional in her home country and married the man of her dreams. Eventually he did studies in another country, his wife and children along, and died unexpectedly of an illness while there. A leader of her husband's clan soon called my friend and told her to come home with her children to perform the traditional widowhood burial rituals. She and her daughters were to have their heads shaved bald in a ceremony before the whole clan. She was to sleep overnight in a thatched hut in the same bed with her husband's dead body. Then she would have sex in that hut with a brother-in-law for ritual cleansing. She would marry her brother-in-law and he would "take over" her children as their father.

If my friend returned to her home country and did not perform these rites, the clan leader threatened, she would bring a curse to the clan and must be killed. She took the threat seriously. A friend of hers had died suspiciously after refusing to perform the long-held traditions. My friend chose not to return home. Her husband's family has now taken all the property she and her husband had both worked to acquire. Culturally, the husband's family was deemed to have authority over the belongings, and my friend (her name is withheld to protect her) received nothing.

Her story is a familiar one in Sub-Saharan Africa – the majority of the continent's land and population, nearly a billion people. Surprisingly, the maltreatment of widows across this vast region has many common themes and causes, but they are not well known internationally. The reasons go deep into the culture.

MEN AT THE TOP

Esther Mombo, the dynamic dean of a university in Africa (one of the few women in such a position), says men in Sub-Saharan Africa are encouraged to see power as dominating and controlling and are "placed at the top." [2] This has existed for centuries, she says, and leads to gender violence. [3]

Nosizo Nakah, a pleasant librarian in Zimbabwe, told me an African man is expected to behave in a certain way. "He is supposed to show he is a man, to behave macho, especially in a traditional African setting. When the man comes home, the children must cower down. His presence is supposed to be felt in the home. The relationship is one of fear for the children and also the lady with the man. It is not a free relationship. The woman becomes part of the man's family – she owns nothing. It is tradition if the husband dies, his family can take everything, including the children if she remarries. So you don't become yourself, your own person. Everything that you do, you have to account to a male partner. So from an African perspective," Nosizo continued, "it's cultural that the widow suffers. The man's family thinks, 'She married into our family. She has now become our wife.' Culturally, this was meant to protect the widow. But I think we've lost it somewhere."

The man's family thinks, 'She married into our family and has now become our wife.'

Nosizo says her husband, Victor, is different – kind and respectful. He has been the African regional director for an international organization, so he is well versed to speak to the issue of male-female relationships on the continent and their effect on widows. "African culture has a lot of positive things – values, virtues, norms," he told me. "But at the end of the day, it is very patriarchal. Of course this is not just the case in Africa. Men are treated better, have more privileges. Sons are treated better. They are seen as the ones to continue the ancestry. The girl child will get married and live in another family, so the parents think, 'Why should we bother?'

"African men traditionally treat their wives as if they are children. These are negatives we cannot run away from. We are born into it. Our fathers model it. If we're not careful, we fall into it. The issue of widows is a follow-through from that.

"A widow thinks, 'Now that my husband has died, how am I going to keep my family together?' All the things the man leaves behind [traditionally] belong to his family, the widow's in-laws. They fear she will give the things to her family. Inheritance laws may say who owns what when someone passes away, but the type of marriage people enter into is what happens when the husband dies. If it's a traditional [tribal] marriage and you are a widow, you could end up living from your small bag."

Laws in various countries may address inheritance issues, he explained, but a traditional, tribal marriage is generally not documented with the government and does not protect the widow. "Even with wills, a woman may have been a housewife. Did she contribute? Yes! But African men generally don't think so. Most men think they are the ones who work, that women are just waiting to receive. In the traditional role the wife belongs to the kitchen. She serves me. With sex, the traditional man says sex is for me. I decide how many children we will have. There is no compromise."

Kenyan Lillian Kimani, who has a doctorate in organizational management, says women in Africa generally have low levels of education and can only get low-paying jobs. Employers don't want to hire them, she says, or let them go to health care and pregnancy clinics. Without a man, a decent job, or Western-style welfare systems, a woman is forced into poverty and maybe even prostitution to care for her children. Kimani confirms that if a husband dies, the wife is often "inherited" by a male relative of her husband. "She can't negotiate."[4]

Such "marriages," where a male relative "inherits" a widow, are almost always polygamous. Generally, African men do not want to marry widows. They may take on a widow out of duty or supposed traditions (some say these are later inventions to justify exploitation),[5] but often, especially in today's context, it is simply to acquire possessions. Such marriages are normally accomplished through traditional rites, with no legal protection.

Polygamous marriages in Sub-Saharan Africa are estimated at 30% of all marriages,[6] although that number is decreasing as the practice becomes less acceptable and more expensive. Instead, affairs on the side are increasing, Victor told me. But this is considered acceptable only for men. Such behavior spreads HIV/AIDS, making widows and then killing many of them too. Lillian Kimani says women may be beaten for even suggesting a man use a condom, because this implies he has been unfaithful.[7]

Beatings of women are common. Jenipha Wasonga, the ebullient director of a counseling center in Kenya, illustrates this fact with a story about a school friend who broke down sobbing one day at school. Finally Jenipha was able to pry out of her friend what was upsetting her so. She was getting breasts, which meant she was becoming a woman, which meant she would be married, which meant she would beaten regularly by her husband someday, like her mother was.[8]

Ifeoma Okoye, a Nigerian author, says the general belief is women are inferior to men and under them, and men should decide what is good or not for women.[9] Perhaps worst of all, women are expected culturally to wear a mask of passivity and not express themselves.[10] This female passivity has been pegged as one of the main factors in the male oppression of women.[11] Surely some progress for women has been made in Africa, and not all women succumb to this pressure. But given the large population that lives in poor rural areas, and the lack of education and economic options for women there, the problem continues.

Compounding women's challenges, most of the land in Africa is controlled by men. Without land, one cannot grow food for one's family, as the vast majority of those in Sub-Saharan Africa do, or have a place for shelter. In Kenya, for example, women are only 5% of registered land owners.[12] Until recently, many African countries did not legally allow women to own land, and some still do not. And changing the law does not instantly change the reality. A woman who lives in a mostly illiterate village, or whose in-laws like tradition as it is, or who has no resources to fight for her rights, is at a distinct disadvantage. And none are more affected by this than the many millions of widows in Africa.

How can a woman inherit property when she herself is property? This is what a Kenyan lawyer was asking when he said in a court of law, now infamously: "How can a chattel inherit a chattel?"[13] A problem landmark ruling by the Supreme Court of Zimbabwe in 1999 found women are not considered adults within a family, but their status is equal to that of teenagers.[14] In many parts of the continent it is still a strong cultural belief that women do not deserve property or cannot be trusted with it, except to raise food for the family.[15] Many women in Africa prove this viewpoint wrong, but the cultural

Women are treated unequally. Some have even called the situation 'gender apartheid.'

belief is still strong. From high courts to humble huts, the traditions often prevail.

Certainly some African societies and individual men have treated women and widows differently. And specific women and widows have responded in a variety of ways, with some faring better than others. But virtually no experts in the field today dispute that women are treated unequally as a gender in Sub-Saharan Africa. Some have even called the situation "gender apartheid."[16]

WIDOWS' DESPERATION

Tradition here says a husband's extended family is supposed to care for his widow and children. But Sub-Saharan Africa is changing. Agricultural land is becoming scarcer. HIV/AIDS has decimated and terrified many communities. Men's and women's roles and responsibilities are not so clear-cut. Men are struggling in their identities as needs and opportunities change.[17] As a result, the fates of widows and their children are often left dangling in the wind.

A Catholic priest in Nigeria, Augustine Okwunna Odimmegwa, did his doctoral work on widows and dedicated it to his two widowed sisters. He says that all too often the brother-in-law just takes the widow's possessions. Then he abandons the accompanying custom to care for the widow and her children.[18] David Kodia, principal of a school in Kenya, says many African men believe they have rights over certain things that have been handed down to them by their forefathers. So they use that tradition to take from widows in ways that are "detrimental to justice and democracy."[19] Even if the widow has worked and contributed to the building of her marital wealth, far too many brothers-in-law (and others in the husband's extended family) like to ignore that fact.

The fates of widows and their children are often left dangling in the wind.

10

The vast majority of men in Sub-Saharan Africa do not have wills, says a Ugandan sociologist.[20] Some fear that a will hastens one's death. And some widows are taught to fear superstitiously that they will die if they inherit land.[21]

The United Nations has estimated that more than 30% of widows and orphans in Sub-Saharan Africa experience illegal property seizure.[22] A recent study of 15 African countries painted a worse picture, finding that more than half of widows do not inherit any assets at all.[23] Without land, or family to assist them, widows have nowhere to grow their family's food, or possibly gain rental income, or even a place to rest their heads for shelter. And education for their children may be out of the question, given costs for required uniforms and books, even in "free" government schools. Daughters especially are kept home to help with other children while the mother tries to find work.

Without a doubt, widows in rural areas, the vast majority of Sub-Saharan Africa, have the worst time of it. They are the least educated and the farthest from options for income generation. Their fate may rest with men who value tribal customs over written law, if such is even known in the villages. Widows who do know their rights may feel powerless to resist. To do so risks ostracism and the possibility of banishment from the village. Community is such a strongly held value in Africa that life without it can seem inconceivable, especially without government safety nets.

Widows who buck community culture and turn to humanitarian organizations for help may pay dearly for doing so. A widow who complained to a human rights lawyer that her brother-in-law had sold all her husband's land, on which she grew her family's food, was reportedly murdered by her in-laws.[24] In fact, murders of widows are reported by various credible sources.[25] Older widows are more likely to be accused of witchcraft, a serious crime that can result in death.[26] Widows Rights International reports an accusation of witchcraft is usually followed by a death sentence.[27] If a widow does survive such accusations, beatings and rape are often part of her life.[28] A considerable number of widows reportedly commit suicide.[29]

No government safety nets such as welfare or food stamps or homeless shelters exist in most of Sub-Saharan Africa. The husband's extended family is supposed to be the safety net for a widow. Friends and family may be too poor to help them. Unless a widow can find gifts of mercy from others, or is one of the small percentage of the population who is fortunate enough to get a microloan for a small business, she and her children are left destitute. Even if a widow can manage to earn a decent living, being single often carries a terrible stigma for her and her children, making them vulnerable to all sorts of attacks.

The cultural emphasis in Africa is on men marrying virgins. So a widow rarely remarries, except to a male relative of her husband, if one will have her. A widow who does not consent to be "inherited," almost always in a polygamous situation, will probably be alone. A life of abject poverty, overwork, and an early death will likely be her lot in life.

The poorest and most exposed widows are those who are old and frail, whose husbands died of HIV/AIDs, who have young children to shelter and feed, or who remain tucked away in refugee and internally displaced camps with no male relative left to accompany them back home, should that option exist. Any war-torn or disease-riddled country, of which there are too many in Africa, leaves a myriad of widows to fend for themselves in the ripped fabric of their societies.

WIDOWHOOD RITUALS

For many widows, the cruelest torment is the rituals they are made to endure immediately after the husband's death. Discussing any traditional African rituals, including those for widowhood, is considered taboo. But a heroic woman from Nigeria who holds her doctorate in education, Patricia Okoye, has written an astonishing book about the humiliations many widows experience.[30] She dedicated it to the memory of her father, a chief, and her newly widowed mother.

Okoye says the widowhood rituals are dehumanizing and can be even more painful than losing land or possessions.[31] They are usually performed by the husband's female relatives, called the *umuada* in parts of her native Nigeria. Open confrontation with this group of relatives, Okoye says, "is tantamount to suicide."[32] And if they do not like the widow, she contends, it is a special chance to vent their anger on her. These shocking rites, as recounted by Okoye and others, can include a wide variety of activities and may be practiced all or in part in various ways by different communities.

One of the most common is scraping off all the widow's body hair in front of others. But other rites may include making the widow:

...Walk naked through the village to a stream
...Sit on the same spot for prolonged periods – sometimes only in a narrow loin cloth
...Wail loudly through the day and night
...Drink water used to bathe her husband's corpse to prove her innocence in his death
...Remain housebound for months
...Wear black in public, if she is allowed out – a huge problem because people do not want to deal with a widow at market or elsewhere for superstitious reasons
...Have 'cleansing sex' with an in-law or outcast to separate her from her husband's spirit
...Keep a fire burning day and night
...Not exit her home after dark
...Not utter a word
...Not shake hands with or touch people
...Not eat with anyone including her children

Widows in Cameroon: "On the celebration day of the deceased husband, the widows move on their buttocks round the celebration ground under the watchful eyes of older widows and sympathizers." Pingpoh Margaret Hongwe, 2004. Widows Rights International.

...Be *caged*, supposedly to protect her from vicious mourners who would throw their whole weight on the widow in the guise of deep sympathy[33]

Caged! My God! The Catholic priest Odimmegwa writes that a progressive traditional chief proclaimed women in his area were no longer to be caged, another confirmation of the practice.[34] Some widows are also reportedly made to crawl to ask forgiveness that their husbands died![35]

How could crawling and the caging of widows possibly be justified culturally? The answer lies in part in the traditional spiritual beliefs of much of Sub-Saharan Africa. A common belief is that the whole community, not just the widow, will come under a curse by the deceased if the widowhood rites are not performed. Only with such rituals can the dead man rest peacefully among his ancestral spirits.[36] A widow may

How could crawling and the caging of widows be justified culturally?

even be forced to undergo "sexual cleansing" with a male relative of her deceased husband, or a village outcast, supposedly to break her spiritual connection with her husband.

Reportedly, countries having the highest incidences of forced sexual cleansing of widows, like Kenya, have the highest reported incidences of HIV/AIDS.[37] So my African friend at the beginning of this chapter was threatened not just with a humiliating and to her immoral ordeal by being told to have sex with her brother-in-law, but also a potentially life-threatening one. Some of those who do survive such widowhood ordeals may still be thrown out of house and home and reduced to begging and prostitution, further spreading diseases like HIV/AIDS. Their daughters may have to follow suit.

Making the widow drink the water used to wash the husband's corpse is one way used to supposedly prove her guilt or innocence in his death. Some forms of traditional African religion contend deaths are not just from physical or natural causes, but have been caused by someone. No police or pathologists investigate many deaths. "Jungle justice"[38] rises to the fore and the widow is often the number-one murder suspect. Common theories are that she may have neglected her husband, used witchcraft, or outright poisoning. In many places, she is considered guilty until proven otherwise.

Broken, perhaps exhausted from nursing a sick husband, the widow faces the rites immediately after the husband's death. Like "hawks on the rampage," Pat Okoye says, the husband's infuriated relatives may swoop down on the hapless widow to avenge his death.[39] Some widows develop mental problems from the trauma.[40] An African news source refers to the "psychological torture" widows experience, leading to depression and health problems.[41] Others use the word "torture" to describe what widows endure, including three published African women theologians, from Kenya, Zambia, and Nigeria.[42] Okoye says if a widow does not complete the expected widowhood rites, the penalties can include death.[43]

The fact that some of Nigeria's states and the country of Ghana have outlawed specific widowhood rites, even some of the most extreme ones listed above, confirms their existence.[44] Ugandan legal scholar Leda Hasila Limann says the importance of widowhood cleansing rituals in many African communities cannot be overstated, and she has called for their criminalization in her country.[45] Few African countries have outlawed such practices, however, far fewer than have addressed property issues for women. And one would be naïve to think that simply outlawing the rites would stop them totally. Further, where police are available, they are often loath to get involved in such cases because they would "interfere with culture." Sometimes, they are simply bribed, as are judges.

HOW WIDESPREAD?

How widespread is the mistreatment of widows across Africa, with humiliating rites and property grabbing? More research is needed by Africans to determine that with more specificity, but numerous African voices, all professionals in their fields, believe the mistreatment of widows is widespread:

IN EVERY AFRICAN SOCIETY
– African theologian[46]

IN MOST AFRICAN COUNTRIES
– Nigerian researcher on widowhood rites[47]

IN ALL OF AFRICA
– Nigerian priest with doctorate on widows[48]

ACROSS THE ENTIRE CONTINENT
– Ugandan legal scholar[49]

IN SUB-SAHARAN AFRICA
– Kenyan researcher[50]

IN MOST AFRICAN COUNTRIES
– Nigerian sociologist[51]

IN MANY PARTS OF SUB-SAHARAN AFRICA
– Ugandan and South African sociologists[52]

MILLIONS TRAUMATIZED
– Nigerian journalist[53]

Echoing this theme, the United Nations claims that regardless of religion, ethnic group, or culture, it is common for widows in Sub-Saharan Africa to be chased from their homes.[54] Widows Rights International states that in many African countries, widows are denied inheritance and land rights as part of a long-term ordeal including loss of "status, livelihood, home, personal safety, and security."[55] The U.S. Congress even has a resolution (championed by an African-American woman legislator) calling the loss of inheritance rights for widows in Africa "a human rights crisis of enormous magnitude" devastating the lives of millions of women.[56] An African magazine calls for a paradigm shift in how Africa as a whole perceives and treats its widows.[57]

Most Sub-Saharan countries keep no statistics on widows, so it's impossible to know how many there are in the region. One estimate suggests that one in four women in Sub-Saharan Africa is a widow.[58] So, based on that figure and the overall population of Sub-Saharan Africa, I estimate this region of the world may have at least 63 million widows, with the majority desperately poor.[59] In the face of the magnitude of widows' suffering on the African continent, and their huge numbers, it is striking that more is not said about them and their plight.[60]

This region may have at least 63 million widows, with the majority desperately poor.

Ironically, more sophisticated women in the cities who are in a better position to speak out for disadvantaged women in their countries are sometimes not fully aware of what the rural women endure, as I discovered in a camp for "internally displaced" people with my highly educated Ugandan host. As one village woman put it, "What do those 'city women' know about our tradition and culture?"[61] In some places, rites are also practiced surreptitiously to prevent interference, while in other, more remote places, interference is not even a consideration.[62]

In fact, general ignorance has existed internationally regarding what many widows in much of Africa suffer. Some have theorized that because far fewer African women than men have been able to engage in academia (funding is often more difficult for women to obtain), such issues, even though they happen across most of Africa, have had few champions who can publish findings. Also, some African women believe if they talk about widows, they themselves will become one, further aggravating the lack of talk about the needs of widows. And the call for a change in rituals, even demeaning ones, can sometimes threaten the very core of a culture. Unless more African voices speak out, significant change will not happen.

As we hear from actual widows in this book, we'll also see some individuals and organizations doing good work for them – fighting for their legal rights, giving them microloans, or simply providing food and offering other acts of mercy. But one thing is clear: *far more work is needed to help Africa's countless widows.*

Can religion help? Africa is considered the world's most religious continent, and a high percentage of its people attend worship services at least once a week.[63] Many of the widows I interviewed mentioned their faith spontaneously, as Africans often do. Further, the vast majority of people in Sub-Saharan Africa profess they are Christians,[64] and the Bible has many strong statements about helping and not hurting widows.

Jesus himself treated widows with special care. So how is the Christian church doing in this area? Can it be a huge force for change regarding widows, and also in the treatment of women

One thing is clear: far more work is needed to help Africa's countless widows.

by men? Or will it use certain Scriptures to reinforce an African culture of male superiority? I consider the actions of the church so critical in this regard that I address the issue more fully in a chapter dedicated to this topic.

In the last chapter we'll look at what can be done by individuals and groups in general to help Africa's countless widows. Here I try to summarize what I have learned. In this chapter, as throughout this book, you'll see I have sought African voices, including the widows themselves and various professionals, for statements of the problem, causes, and solutions. It has been my privilege to do so.

Space does not permit telling the stories of the more than 60 widows I have interviewed, but the following chapters give the stories I consider most representative. Only a few stories that duplicated themes already shared in a chapter were eliminated. The last names of most widows, and even the first names of some, are withheld to protect them. As we go, I give some background on each country where I interviewed widows. I also describe some of what it took for me to find them, and what it was like meeting with them in huts and refugee camps, black townships and crowded markets.

I have also added one other feature to this book. Most of the widows I met conveyed their stories with much dignity and lack of self-pity, with some breaking and weeping only when they could contain themselves no more. So I composed a brief story for the end of each chapter, fiction but inspired by fact, to hopefully bring the enormous plight of African widows, and what needs to be done, more alive to the reader. After all, stories are a major part of the African way of communicating. You will see these fiction pieces edged by a border of African cloth to set them off. As I wrote them, I myself often broke and wept, and they flowed from me as if I were actually witnessing the scenes.

Not every widow in Africa experiences such wretched circumstances as some described in this book, but countless millions of African widows do, and their stories of heartbreak and courage need to be told.

In the next chapter we begin our journey to seven African countries in Rwanda. But first, a story...

RISING IN RIGHTEOUSNESS

We are the *umuada*, daughters of the land. Women of the dead man. Through the ancestors, our blood mingled warm and hot with his. His wife, our wife, is the stranger here today. She is not a daughter of the land. Her blood is not same with ours.

So today, we hold the big stick of power. Some of us are drunk with it, like men who drink palm wine till it almost pours out their ears.

We have swarmed to the widow like giant bees to sweet, sticky honey. What does she have? What can be taken? So little is left after the men come and take the land and cooking pots and other things. But what is left is her soul. Some of us want a piece of that.

When my husband died, it was not so. I was one who received kindness. His sisters and aunts and nieces were kind to me. Their gentleness warmed me like a good sun. I loved them even more after that. We became like true sisters.

But this *umuada* today is a web woven by enemies. Like a cloth with bad stains on a beautiful pattern. And the black is spreading as others listen to lies about this widow.

I know her. I have lived in this same village with her since I married a man from here. She could not have killed her man. She is kind and good. No dark rivers run in her heart.

The *umuada* have gathered now. They sit in a circle. The widow sits naked in the middle. And I am here too, in this circle I do not like.

We will decide if she is guilty of murdering her husband. He died of a long sickness. Did she poison him? She will be asked that today. She has just said goodbye to him. She loved him. I know that. He was not a perfect man. But she loved him.

It begins. I see her try to make herself strong, like the giant tree with rippling leaves that grows by the river. But soon she weeps like the African willow tree. The betrayal is too strong for her. It breaks her like a bad man breaking a stick over his thigh before he beats his wife with it.

It is the strong, mean one who asks most of the questions. Who points her finger many times at the widow. She is the oldest sister to the dead man and was once married to a chief in another village. I heard the chief was a bad man. He beat her and her children every night. One, a boy, died in the hiding place of banana leaves she built in the bush for her children when they ran from him. The wounds to the boy's body were too great for his gentle heart to heal. After that, a wildness came into her eyes. When her husband died, she was accused of poisoning him. Maybe that was true.

I heard she was made to sit on the same pile of ashes for months, that she would scream from the ants who found their way inside her flimsy loin cloth. The leaders of the *umuada* she faced smiled then. They said she is screaming for her lost husband, our brother. But that was not true. She was never the same.

Now today it is she who holds the bad stick of power. Her eyes glint like a machete that has been sharpened for a long time. My eyes want to turn away.

But look they must. This widow has been good to me. She comforted me when my husband died. Her daughter has cared for me with tenderness when I was sick and I have called her my granddaughter.

Today the *umuada* must speak with one voice. It is tradition. The strongest women speak out and the weaker ones stay silent. Or they too could suffer terrible things if they speak up to the strong ones. I am not one of those. I have always let my voice be silent in the groups. And I am old now.

But I cannot be silent today.

I struggle to stand. My knees hurt from the effort to rise alone. I think of how the widow's daughter always runs to help me when she sees me trying to get to my feet. But she cannot be here, in this group that will decide about her mother. The memory comes to me now, like a warm comfort, how she has rubbed oils into my knees for me when they hurt the worst. Yes, I must do this thing. For her, and for her mother. Heads turn to me as I struggle to stand. All eyes of the *umuada* are on me.

"I know this widow," I say. "I have lived in this village with her and my eyes that have now grown old have watched her. She cared for her husband with goodness and kindness. She could not have poisoned him."

A ripple of fear went through the circle. Eyes turned to the woman who had been trying to make her voice rule. My eyes watch her carefully too. I see the new widow looks also. I almost see with my fading old eyes a little white bird of hope begin to flutter in her heart.

All the *umuada* know we must be of one voice. And now my voice has dared to fly out of my mouth to speak different words. I watch the hardened sister to the dead man. I feel my eyes became strong and fierce, much stronger than my old knees that struggle to hold up my body. Where did I find such courage, I wonder? But then I know. The goodness of the widow and her daughter cannot be forgotten. It helps me to stand inside my heart.

The women sitting in the group look down, away from me and the leader. They adjust their bodies a little. Then, finally, like a flash of sun coming out from a dark cloud, the sister to the dead man smiles. It is a good smile, not a bad one. A smile of surrender to what is true. To the kindness her heart had long needed. "You are right, *Mma*. You know her best. You have lived here in the same village. We will listen to you. This widow will have a shorter grieving time on the ground and we will cover her nakedness."

A wave of relief flows through my heart like the sudden winds of a cooling summer storm. I know I have done what should be done. Now I can die in peace. This good widow who cared for me so many times, and her kind daughter, have been spared much grief.

PART I

WIDOWS' STORIES

MOROCCO

TUNISIA

ALGERIA

LIBYA

EGYPT

WESTERN SAHARA

MAURITANIA

MALI

NIGER

CHAD

SUDAN

ERITREA

DJIBOUTI

GAMBIA

SENEGAL

GUINEA
BISSAU

GUINEA

BURKINA FASO

BENIN

TOGO

NIGERIA

SOUTH
SUDAN

ETHIOPIA

SIERRA
LEONE

COTE
D'IVOIRE

GHANA

LIBERIA

CENTRAL AFRICAN
REPUBLIC

SOMALIA

CAMEROON

EQUATORIAL
GUINEA

GABON

CONGO REPUBLIC

DEMOCRATIC
REPUBLIC OF
THE CONGO

UGANDA

KENYA

RWANDA

BURUNDI

CABINDA

TANZANIA

ANGOLA

ZAMBIA

MALAWI

COMOROS

ZIMBABWE

MOZAMBIQUE

MADAGASCAR

NAMIBIA

BOTSWANA

SWAZILAND

LESOTHO

SOUTH
AFRICA

NORTH AFRICA

SUB-SAHARAN
AFRICA

2

UNDER RWANDA'S SPREADING UMINYINYA TREE

"In this country, to have family is like a miracle."

Abakunda Odeth, Rwandan who helps widows

Rwanda. Land of a thousand hills and many more widows. Genocide. Destroyer of societies. Widow maker. Nearly 50,000 from the 1994 genocide alone.[1]

And yet, when I went to Rwanda, I had no idea I would love it so much. Yes, the history sears. Many are still haunted by their experiences. But the people have found the strength to move on, to rebuild a better country. The widows too have found fresh courage to care for their remaining children and the children of those no longer here.

The physical beauty of Rwanda can be astounding. You stand breathless on a hilltop at the sight of a lake ringed with old volcanic peaks. Perhaps you wonder, have I ever seen anything this beautiful?

Rwanda. Landlocked. The most densely crowded country in Africa. Too many people, not enough room. Not enough land to feed everyone. Factions form. Tempers flare. Old allegiances do not die.

But people do. One to two million in 90 days.[2] Soldiers and gangs of one tribe roam the streets and kill people of the other tribe. About 20% of the country's population is decimated. A million more people flee as refugees, taking nothing with them, into neighboring countries. Land is seized unscrupulously from many, including widows and orphans.

At that time, women were not allowed to own land in Rwanda. After the genocide, a new law changed that. And Rwanda became the only country in the world where women are the majority of the parliament.

The President of Rwanda at this writing, Paul Kagame, is intentionally gender inclusive. This same President personally marched into Rwanda during the genocide to liberate it from the perpetrators. And this is the President who is now world-renown for his many actions to make his country one of the safest and fastest-growing economically in Africa.

When this President was a toddler, a biographer says, he and his family had literally run from killers in the earlier genocide of 1959.[3] They were related to the queen of Rwanda, and her driver swerved up in her car to rescue the family on a hillside just as they were about to be caught and murdered. They then fled to neighboring Uganda, where they lived as refugees. The future president had schooling under a tree with only a stick to scratch his letters and numbers on his leg, and a father embittered by his fate.

Kagame's whole upbringing, which later included military training and being a guerilla fighter, focused on returning to Rwanda and reclaiming it as his homeland once again. When finally he marched with soldiers back into Rwanda to liberate her from those widow-

and-orphan makers, it was as if his whole life had been designed for this.[4]

For years after the genocide, justice was sought in thousands of "gacaca courts," the ancient Rwandan tradition of a community gathering under the shade of a large tree to settle village disputes. At one point, the government still had more than 100,000 accused war criminals awaiting trial, with some estimates much higher. The courts were overwhelmed, and the government officially sanctioned the gacaca courts to deal with genocide crimes, including murder and rape. If a criminal confessed before his village, the penalties were less. With no confession and witnesses who would speak out, the penalties were more. Those who lost family members—spouses, children, parents, siblings—had a chance to speak, to rail, to weep, hopefully to see justice served. Then all were expected to try to forgive, to move on, to heal, as individuals and as a country.

On a prior visit to Rwanda in 2009, the car I was in passed a solemn group gathered under a tree. The driver confirmed it was a gacaca court.

"Can we stop?" I asked.

"You must have permission in advance to attend a gacaca," he replied somberly. "Outsiders can disrupt the proceedings. They can disturb the comfort of the victims and witnesses and criminals to speak out." I understood but was disappointed. The gacaca courts for the genocide would soon be ceasing. It was time to move on for the victims and the country. As an outsider I had no right to sit in, but I wanted to hear and share the stories of genocide widows.

WAR WIDOWS

A Rwandan named Jane (pronounced Jah-nay) was widowed in 1994. She was 34, with three children. When the genocidaires came to her neighborhood, everyone scattered, she said, running, hiding

29

in different places, hiding in the bushes, hiding with children, trying to keep the crying children quiet while they hid. Jane ran with her baby boy already strapped on her back, as is common with African women, and with her daughter. They ran to the high grasses on the terracing where cows would feed. They hid among the feces from the animals. They survived to tell the story.

When I met Jane, her beauty, even at age 52, impressed me. She had wrapped a sky blue turban with a bit of shine to it artfully around her head, highlighting her high cheek bones. Hers, I thought, was the kind of face world-class photographers want for magazine covers. She had a lovely figure too and moved with feminine elegance. Her smile was winsome, and her manner captivating. It was a joy to be around her. Jane never remarried, like the vast majority of Africa's widows.

Jane

She ushered us graciously into her home. I was impressed when I saw her house from the exterior because it was more than a small one or two-room home. When we walked into the living room, though, there were only four wooden chairs and a simple wooden coffee table. No cushions, no rugs, nothing on the walls. I found out by talking to Jane that this was a house President Kagame had built. He'd found out that widows of the tribe persecuted in '94 were still having their homes torched by people of the persecuting tribe, years after the genocide.

This had happened not once, but twice to Jane's home. At night, she told me, people who knew her would throw stones at the house. That was a warning for her to get out before trouble came.

In the morning, she would leave the home to save her life and the lives of her children. Then the house with everything in it would be burned.

When President Kagame found out this was happening to widows, he was angry.

"When President Kagame found out this was happening to widows," Jane said, "he was angry." He came himself to her community to meet with the local leaders. He asked them why this was still happening to genocide survivors. Then he had the government build houses for genocide widows like Jane.

But like many of the truly poor, widows and their children don't always have water or food to eat. "Sometimes in this house," Jane explained in her Kinyarwandan language and my interpreter told me, "We don't have 20 francs [about 3 cents U.S. currently] to fetch water." She grows some crops: beans, cassava, maize. Her daughter is looking for a job. The day before, the daughter had gone to the people digging the road nearby to see if she could get work. Jane's two sons are still students and not yet able to get jobs.

The baby boy she ran with on her back, 18 at our visit, came into the home where we were meeting. He put his arm around his mother lovingly and greeted her guests warmly and courteously, with handshakes all around in the Rwandan tradition. He obviously loved and respected his mother and also had some of his mother's charisma. All others in her extended family, and her husband's family, had died in the genocide. She has no relatives, she said, to ask for help.

A Rwandan woman in her 30s brought me to meet Jane. Odeth Abakunda, or in the Rwandan tradition with last name first, Abakunda Odeth, is on staff with Youth With A Mission (YWAM).[5] Odeth visits about 250 widows on a regular basis, helping them with crucial needs, starting small businesses, and taking time to talk with them about their lives as she did today.

Odeth and Jane greeted each other warmly when we arrived and began to catch up a bit with each other in their shared language. I was surprised then to see Jane, previously so poised, start to tear up. Odeth stopped to tell me in English that Jane had visited a memorial for the genocide. It was April, Odeth explained, an annual time of mourning for the Rwandans because this is the month when the mass killing began.

At the memorial Jane visited, many skulls are lined up artfully in tribute to those who died. I had been to that memorial with my friend Tom Allen, who left Southern California after 30 years of law practice to live a life of service in Rwanda. When we went to the memorial, it was wrenching. At one point I felt nauseous seeing so many skulls of murdered people, artfully and respectfully displayed.

But for Jane to visit such a memorial? "She wondered if one of the skulls was her mother who was killed in the genocide," Odeth translated. "My mother was beautiful and had a tall nose," Jane said. "I would look at the skulls and think, 'Maybe that one is my mom.' When I came back home, I was sick."

That wasn't the only time Jane showed courage. After her husband was killed, she was determined to recover his body, even though it was dangerous. Jane was told many bodies, including her husband's, were buried together in a big hole dug in the ground. Somehow she was able to go there, find his body and return it to his land for burial, an important tradition in Africa.

Jane leads a widows' group in her community. "It's difficult to be a widow when you have no other person to tell," she said through Odeth. Some of the widows are even from the other ethnicity that murdered her relatives. "To see your friends, your neighbors you share milk with, who give you cows and you share what you have, that they are the ones who kill you, kill your husband, it shocked me," Jane said. "I became hopeless, I was quiet, I didn't want to talk with anyone. I was a Christian, but it was only me and God. I didn't care about anyone."

When Jane was young, she said, conflicts between ethnicities were going on then too. "My father was beaten and he died. I was smart in school, number one in my class, but because I was an orphan [considered such culturally, even if you have a mother], and because we were the persecuted tribe, I was not allowed to go to secondary school. Even when I was young, I was not happy."

After the genocide, Rwandans from YWAM came to her community hoping to start a widows' group and help them. Widows from both tribes were invited, those whose husbands were killed, and those who had done the killing. "You had to look at the ones whose husbands did the killing," Jane said. "I didn't want to talk with them. I know widows whose husbands killed people. I didn't want to see them. I came to the first meeting, but I stayed home the second meeting. YWAM came to my home to see why and encouraged me to come, so I came to the third meeting."

The widows were encouraged to choose a leader and chose Jane, even the women from the other tribe. When Jane came home, she was thinking, "How can I hate these people? They want me to be their leader. To know your husband killed is shame for them.

"After they chose me, I started to love them, because they loved me. Also, YWAM was teaching forgiveness, unity, reconciliation, repentance. That's when my heart began to open, to love others. Before that, I was dead. I was walking, but I was dead. I was like an animal. I used to have heart problems, pain in my heart, it was beating, beating, beating a lot. But now I don't have that. YWAM came to me, they loved me. Now I have other people. I lost my family, but I have others near me."

At the end of our interview, I asked Jane about her dreams, what she hopes to do now. She replied immediately that she wants to arrange a big conference for widows. She wants to tell them how God will provide, not to be begging and feeling helpless, but to rely on God. "When you are a widow, you can feel useless, you get no respect, you feel hopeless. Some people stay in their houses. But I want to tell people how God is a husband, a father to the fatherless."[6] Clearly, Jane was a visionary. "Half of the women here are widows," she explained. "Twenty-eight are from the genocide, but many more had their husbands die other ways."

Many were stuck in their pain and needed someone to reach out to them, especially those who had family die in the genocide. Odeth emphasized it is traditional for family to help, and if the husband's family are good people, they will help you. "But in this country to have family is like a miracle. Many families have died. And if they are living, many are poor."

After Jane, I met with numerous other widows in her neighborhood to hear their stories, some widowed by the genocide and some by other causes. But one I particularly liked had been honored by President Kagame for raising six orphaned children. He named her a "Malayika Murinzi," an Angel Protector. Phelomena came to Jane's home to meet with us because the rains of the night before had made the way to her home quite muddy. Jane waited outside her own home to give Phelomena privacy while we spoke inside.

Phelomena was age 58, with an air of wisdom about her. All her own children and her husband died in the genocide. Her husband's family and hers were all killed too, except for one brother who is sickly with diabetes. She teared up with worry talking about him. The government built her a house too as a genocide widow. It also pays school fees for the five children of the persecuted ethnicity she raises, but not for one boy of the other ethnicity in her home.

When you are a widow, you can feel useless, you get no respect, you feel hopeless.

During the war, she told me, she ran with her baby to a neighbor she trusted who was of the persecuting tribe and asked him to hide them. "I cannot hide you because they will kill me too," he told her, "but I will pray for you." Phelomena said it meant a lot to her that he would pray for her. She said she was not offended he would not hide her. She would never forget him.

After that she ran into the "bush-bush," as Odeth translated it, with a baby girl of four months. There she saw a "bright kind of rainbow." She felt like God was showing her through the rainbow the way to go. She hid for a whole week and survived, but all of her family were killed. Her tone and gestures grew dramatic as she told her story. "Our families died, but they did nothing," she said. "They were innocent." They put them in latrines, she added sorrowfully.

Something rose up in me, and knowing she was a Christian, I told her with conviction that her family didn't stay in those latrines--they were in heaven now! She began to weep, a good kind of crying, the releasing kind. She wiped her tears on a corner of the cloth wrapped around her hips, yet another use for that ubiquitous wrap. And there would be six families in heaven, I added, who would run to her when she arrived there, surrounding her with hugs and kisses, thanking her for raising their children, and telling her she was part of their families now too. She would have much family in heaven, I told her. Her countenance began to lift.

After a bit, she continued. "My prayer now is to help my children finish their schools, to get nice husbands who love them, so when I die my kids will be in their homes and not around. I pray what happened in '94 will never happen again." She is close with the children. "The girls do not go after boys," she said with obvious pride.

Then she added, "What I would like to do is teach the widows to be women of integrity and to accept who they are, to give all their burdens to God." As we wrapped up our time together, she

35

thanked me for coming. She wants to talk, she said, but has no one to talk to. "Before we talked," she added, "my heart was heavy, but now… it is light." We walked joyfully together out of Jane's house into the sunlight.

Jane was waiting for us under the covered area outside her front door with several friends. Another widow who also wanted to talk to me was there too. But Odeth and I were worn out. We'd talked to numerous widows by then, and the last one was quite emotional. Odeth was tired from the intensity of translating for hours, and I from writing (I never trust recording equipment totally). But Dapholose, a widow of 52 years, had been waiting for us, so we agreed to speak with her there outside Jane's front door. Her story turned out to be one of the most dramatic I'd heard, and so dark I almost didn't include it here.

The husband of Dapholose and two of her children had been killed in the genocide, and for a long while she didn't know what had happened to her third child, a girl of six. Dapholose didn't know for sure if this child had even survived. She would ask people repeatedly if her daughter had come back to where they had lived. Then Dapholose got word her daughter was there.

Dapholose learned from her daughter that she had been taken during the war to neighboring DR Congo. There she was raped repeatedly from ages six to eight. One day she was put in a burlap bag, wrapped up, and left in the bush. Some local defenses came along and saw this bag with something shaking in it. They opened it and raped her too. She was raped so badly she could not sit and had to lean against a tree. Blood would run out of her. Finally, she was taken by someone to the Red Cross in the DR Congo. Eventually, two years after the genocide, she came back to Rwanda with a group of returning refugees. When mother and daughter were finally reunited, the daughter's

'Before we talked,' she added, 'my heart was heavy, but now… it is light.'

feet would not work and her fingernails were gone. She seemed small to her mother and darker in color than before.

Dapholose worked hard to earn money to take her daughter to the hospital. Now she is graduating from senior 6 in school, quite an accomplishment. But she is traumatized every April, the public anniversary of the genocide. "Everybody was raped," Dapholose said "even me." But obviously she had not been destroyed, and had fought to give her daughter renewed life. It was an honor to meet her.

Another widow, whom I met several days later, not through Odeth, told me she too was beaten, raped, and infected with HIV/AIDS during the war. The men would tell her to throw her baby away and then rape her. Afterward, she would go find her baby. That daughter is now 19 with many problems, the widow now in her late 30s. She said she has emotional problems, putting her head down briefly to recover herself.

After her husband was killed in the genocide, she wanted to live on the land of her husband's family, according to tradition. But because her marriage had not been registered (she was married young to a neighbor in the traditional fashion), the government could not help her gain access to the land. Most of her own family was killed in the genocide and those who lived, including two sisters who are also widows, are poor.

She married again, but that husband died of kidney problems. Sometimes now she gets work building houses, but it is tiring for her. She takes ARVs (Anti-Retroviral drugs for the HIV/AIDS), which she gets through an association in Rwanda for the widows of the genocide.[7]

"Do you know of many other widows?" I asked her. She nodded yes, of course she does.

"Do you go to a church?" I asked, concerned if she had community support from somewhere given her beaten-down manner. "Yes," she replied, "without praying I can easily die." I wished then she knew Odeth and was in Jane's group of widows.

Odeth, only in her early 30s, told me how she had decided to start working with widows. "I was not in Rwanda during the genocide," she said. "My parents left in '59 [during the prior time of killing the same tribe], but we came back in '94 right after the genocide.

"The place was full of bodies. It smelled bad. We were on a tea plantation. We didn't know where to walk for the bodies. From '94 to '96, people in Uganda, Kenya, and Tanzania didn't eat fish because the bodies from Rwanda were in the lakes. There were even bodies on the roofs. I was 15.

"My parents came back because they were tired of being refugees, even me. You had to change your name if you were Rwandan. If you were taking exams, they wouldn't give you marks. When we got back here, we started a house, gardening, had some cows. Life was good, to have your own nation. After finishing senior 6th, I came here to Kigali to find a job. My cousin did training with YWAM and encouraged me to do the same. During my training, God told me to work with widows and orphans."

When we returned to the YWAM base, Odeth showed me a little shop she had organized there with handicrafts made by widows. The widows are trained how to make beautiful beaded jewelry and baskets. Some micro-loans are offered to the widows so they can sell bananas and avocados. There's also a little mushroom-growing shed as an experiment to see if that might be a good business for the widows. "There's a good market for mushrooms," Odeth said with entrepreneurial spirit.

At this writing, Odeth and Jane are working on Jane's dream of a conference for widows.

JUSTICE BATTLES

International Justice Mission (IJM) has done amazing work defending the legal rights of the oppressed on multiple continents, including Africa.[8] Part of their work has been defending widows who have their land taken away upon the husband's death. In Rwanda I met one of their clients, a brave widow named Theresa. Together we sat in a clearing under a large, spreading uminyinya tree that was in the front yard of the IJM offices. Throughout Rwanda, trees like this one have provided shady gathering places.

Theresa seemed tired. She told me through our IJM translator that she was ill with HIV/AIDS and sleeping outside at night in front of her home. Her mother-in-law had taken the home after her son's death and, according to Theresa, hoped she would die before reclaiming it. But Theresa wanted the land for her children and would not go away. She told me her story up to that point, but it was hard to follow. Two years later, I met her once again. I thought it was the wrong person. This woman was in an African-patterned dress and turban with a professional air and wore nice sandals with silver trim and wire-rim glasses. She had a sparkle and vitality about her.

"Do you remember me?" I asked her doubtfully. "Yes!" she replied through the IJM staff member who was translating. "But you look different!" I exclaimed. She smiled. "That's because my land has been restored to me! And I'm a bank teller now! I'm on ARVs [Anti-Retrovirals for the HIV/AIDS], and it works good!" Then she told me her story from sad beginning to success. "When my husband was still living and I

Theresa

39

realized I was HIV positive, it was a hard thing to accept. I wasn't responsible for that. Also, I was looking at the children, thinking they would be orphans.

"So I asked my husband's mother to come along, to help nurse my husband. I felt I was to be there for him. I told her, and she thought that was admirable. We let her stay on one of the two lands we had worked to get, as long as we had the other one. But we were not giving it to her.

"When my husband died, he left a lot of loans. I knew that was my responsibility, but I was getting weak. I lost my job. The bank said it would sell the house to get back their money. I was destroyed by that. I had worked so hard. This house was for my children. I thought there was no way that could happen. I thought I could go live with my husband's mother. She was living in our three-bedroom house. On the same land was a small house too. I could rent that out to someone and pay the loan with that.

"When I went to my mother-in-law, she said, 'No, no, my son has given me this house! No way can you live with me!' She was quite angry and said bad words like, 'Why didn't you die like your husband?' Then she said I could live in the small, one-bedroom place with my children. I went to the local leaders to ask them to help me get my property back. They said we should live together, but my husband's mother refused. She kept saying it was her property.

"I had a document showing the house was mine, the marriage certificate, every document that is needed. She had no documents the land was hers, but one of the local leaders was a friend to her, and her niece was powerful. There was a bit of injustice. They told me to find another place. I

They told me to find another place. I say I have no place to go. This is my property. I will stay.

say, 'I have no place to go. This is my property. I will stay.'

"There was a big conflict with the local leaders. My husband's mother was playing like she was a victim. To me she was angry and said my children were not from her son. My son and I eat and sleep outside. I was falling sick often because of the conditions. I was sad and discouraged. I had already become a widow, but I was mentally prepared for that. When he died, life was hard. But when I was losing the properties we had both worked for, I felt lost completely. I had lost all we built for our children. Then I really felt like a widow.

"Then a woman at the hospital told me about an organization that helps widows. It was IJM. They decided to help me. They said my case needed to be fought in court."

IJM fought for Theresa through four years and four appeals by the mother-in-law. Theresa won repeatedly. Then the mother-in-law hid, so she could not be removed from the main house to live in another house. Her niece would say Theresa had kidnapped her. IJM went to the police and resolved that too. IJM also spearheaded the process to get the land registered by Rwanda's national land center in Theresa's name.

When Theresa finished her story, I told her women in other countries would be inspired by her courage. She had fought for the land to give her children an inheritance, even sleeping outside on it at night while sick with HIV/AIDS for three months in her battle. What strength she had to persist for four years through the battles and not give up!

After Theresa and I finished our time together, then Beatrice, an old blind woman, was brought to meet with me. Her eyes were covered over with skin. She was dressed in a bright African cloth wrapped around her body in the old style rather than a fitted outfit. She had a head scarf of blue and yellow and was quite striking. A young woman, probably a relative, led her to meet with me with our translator, Chantal. Beatrice carried a branch carved to be a walking stick. She carried her identity card in a paper bag saying she was 58, but to me she looked much older.

Chantal stepped quickly out of the pleasant room to bring some tea for them. Perhaps they had not had any sustenance yet that day. Beatrice, the young woman with her, and I did not share a language and the silence became awkward. I began to sing a gentle song to help put the two women at ease. I'm not the best singer, but it was all I knew to do.

Soon Chantal returned, and I asked if Beatrice would say a prayer for our interview in her language. I wanted her to feel like she was in a position of leadership for a few moments, and I also valued her prayers. Beatrice prayed in her language with great strength and had a powerful presence. I said thank you in the Kinyarwanda language, and we all laughed at my poor attempt at their pronunciation. In that moment,

Beatrice

a beautiful smile lit up Beatrice's life-beaten face. I learned later she had been blinded as a young pregnant woman by a landmine left from the '94 killings.

Beatrice was not technically a widow. Her husband was in prison for supposed genocide crimes and will probably die there. "Many women have husbands in prison for life," Chantal explained, "or for such long sentences that, considering the conditions in prison and that some are HIV-positive, they have no hope their husbands are coming back alive. Or they may be gone in the forest somewhere as beggars, but the wives don't know where they are. They consider themselves widows."

IJM had helped Beatrice to regain a piece of land from her family.

I saw jungle, felt the darkness. I sure don't want to go there, I thought.

Other justice battles were being waged by a legal aid clinic in western Rwanda that also helps poor individuals with land issues. Gilbert Mwenedata, a staff member for USAID (the United States Agency for International Development), which was funding the clinic in part, invited me to come along for a site check. On the two-hour drive, he told me land rights are related to 70% of all disputes in Rwanda. Most of those needing help with this issue, he said, are women. People who will speak out for individuals in court, like those at this free clinic, are in great demand.

When we drove into the small town that held the clinic, we passed by the border crossing to the Democratic Republic of the Congo (DRC). It was only a small booth for officials to check documents and a wooden vehicle arm with painted stripes where vehicles could pass. I looked across the border at the DRC, the "rape capital of the world." I saw jungle, felt the darkness. I sure don't want to go there, I thought.

Then I noticed a nice-looking young woman, who evidently had just passed through the border into Rwanda, walking along slowly. She had a dazed look, as if she'd really suffered. I've since heard one often sees this look on the women who come from eastern DRC.

At the clinic we heard heartbreaking stories. One woman hadn't seen her seven-year-old child since her husband abandoned her and took the child away. This is the man's right according to tradition in Sub-Saharan Africa. We also heard a distressing story from a brave 18-year-old who was caring for her four younger siblings the best she could after their parents sold the family land and abandoned them. Then we heard from a widow whose children tried to survive on the streets after she grew weak with HIV/AIDS, and whose stepbrother wouldn't let them live on her father's land. Everyone waiting at the clinic hoped to find some justice. But only some of them had strong enough cases to receive legal help.

WIDOW'S DAUGHTER

My last interview in Rwanda was with the daughter of a widow. Her family had fled from Rwanda during the '59 war. She had been born in the DR Congo, where she and her family also saw fighting and war.

Claudine was considered an orphan because her father had died, reputedly from poisoning by a relative through marriage who wanted his land. This is not unusual, she said. Her mother then sold things at the market like potatoes and beans, and Claudine was able to go to school. Then after the '94 genocide, when refugees began returning to Rwanda, she rode with her mother and siblings in a little truck back from the Congo. Three years later, her mother died. Claudine and all her siblings then went to different families.

"What should be done for widows?" I asked her through a friend who was translating.

"Help them to raise the children," she replied without hesitation. "Put them through school. I loved studying." Then she choked up. I was surprised. Claudine was strong. She did not hesitate to tell the men who worked on the yard of the home where she worked as a maid what to do. Then she regained her composure and explained that after her mother died, there was not enough money for her to even buy notebooks for school. She was forced to quit.

"I still have a dream to study accounting," she said, "and I am

44

saving my money to take classes at night and on weekends." This is especially admirable given that she has several children of her own. She is probably in her late 20s.

I still have a dream to study accounting. I am saving my money to take classes.

"When the husbands die," she added, "it's important the families give freedom to the women, help them, visit them, because you need support when you're a widow. The husband's family usually threatens the woman and wants the house back where she lived. A sister could come and say, 'It's my brother's house. It's mine. I cannot let it go.' She may say, 'I want my brother's things back.' I know many families this happens to. It happens to most widows."

After my interview with Claudine, my time in Rwanda was done. I'd met such amazing widows and the daughter of one. After a full day of meetings, I boarded an 8 p.m. flight for a short, 45-minute jaunt to the capital of Uganda, and then on for the long journey to Brussels, where I would make my next connection. When I sat down, I noticed a professional-looking African woman, probably in her mid-30s, in the seat next to me by the window. Should I speak with her, I wondered, or close my eyes for a rest?

Before I knew it, we were talking pleasantly. Soon I found out she was an attorney working for the United Nations on women's land issues in Uganda. In fact, she was on her way back from Geneva where she had spoken at a U.N. conference on the topic. I told her about my Master's thesis and work on women's land issues, including how widows were affected. We were both stunned that our work had such similarities, especially in a field where not many people were working, and here we were sitting next to each other on a plane.

What were the odds that we would be seated next to each other on this short 45-minute flight and happen to talk? Pretty slim, we both knew. Before that 45-minute flight was over, Deborah invited me to come to Uganda. She would take me into the refugee camps, she said, to meet the women she worked with. Would that really materialize, I wondered?

But next, I would go to Ghana, where I would meet the widow who told me her story about "half a piece of cloth."

BORDER CROSSING

I can't believe they did it again. I never wanted to go back, to give them another chance at me. But then I got the call about my mother. She is dying. She is screaming in pain. I am the only one who can bring the medicine. No one else has any money. No one can get the medicine to ease her pain. She has the slow death from the bad disease that eats away at the body.

I've heard that in rich countries poor people can get medical help free. But not in Congo. It is hard even to get to a hospital. And you cannot enter without money. They let you die outside their door instead. One more body to throw away.

All night after the call about my mother, I tossed on my mattress like a flopping fish on the bank of the big river. My mother. The one who nursed me when I was sick. The one who never complained when she was sick.

And now she was screaming in pain? I could not bear it. I could not stay away. But only for her would I walk back into that hell where she lives.

Why wouldn't she come with me when I left? She knew I had to go! How could I stay? Those wicked men who ruined me. The hole they put in my body. The terrible smell. The leaking of pee and poops. No man would want me then.

The kind doctor at the hospital fixed many women. He talked gently to women he could not fix. We all lay in a big room together, smelling each other's terrible smells, listening to each other's prayers, singing a strong song when a surgery worked, crying together when it didn't. Not every woman could be fixed. Some were too badly torn.

But I was one he could fix! He gave me a new life. I could almost live like a normal person again. The smell was gone. I met a man in Rwanda after I came back here for a new life. He looked at me with kindness and a shine in his warm eyes. He had been ruined too, in a way. His heart had been ruined.. .by the genocide. He saw his family killed. He was one who hid

47

and was not found. He did not need a perfect wife. I hoped we would marry.

Then I got the call about my mother in Congo. She needed me. I did not want to leave the man. Maybe I could not return to him if I left. But my mother was in terrible pain. I was the only one to help her. I missed her too. I wanted to see her again one more time before she went into the home of heaven. Put my arms around her like a child one last time.

The man understood. But he was afraid for me. He could not come with me. He would be killed for sure. People in my mother's village knew him. The bad soldiers nearby had run from Rwanda when Kagame came marching in to stop the killing. They would finish my good man. They would butcher him.

Only I could go. Maybe I could slip in and out of Congo. I could kiss my mother one more time and ease her pain. I knew I would feel bad the rest of my life if I did not help her. I tossed and turned some more like a fish with a hook in its mouth. My hook was the worry for my mother. Couldn't she have a good death after all she did for me and many others? These bad dreams I was having. . .her calling to me. . .her face filled with pain. I had to go.

I bought the medicine, the strong one for dying. It cost everything I had saved and more to buy it. Then I had to pay money for the ferry to reach my mother across the big lake. The man gave me what he had saved too. That really touched me. I hated to take it and only did so for my mother.

I walked across the border from Rwanda into Congo. I kept telling myself I would be back in Rwanda soon.

Finally I arrived at my mother's little hut. I felt her love when I saw her. Maybe an angel was there to watch over her in her dying. But I was her angel today. The angel with medicine in my hands.

I was tired down to my bones. And I was shocked. My mother had changed so much. I know coming death changes people. But at first I wondered if this was my mother. Then I moved closer to her. Yes, it was my mother! I fell to my knees by her bed and

kissed her face all over. I took her hands and kissed them too.
I put one to my chest. I wanted her to feel my heart beating.

She had done that many times when I was a child. She
told me her heart was beating with love for me. She knew why
I put her hand to my heart. A little smile crossed her face. Till
she screamed out in pain again, unable to stop herself.

Quickly as I could I prepared the medicine for her. I
dropped the powder in a little bottle of water I had and held
her chin as I poured it down her throat as carefully as I could.
I didn't want to spill a drop.

Soon she was sleeping peacefully. My old aunty nodded
her head at me. She looked so tired. She had carried my
mother's pain with her in her heart while she cared for her.
She looked much older too. She would probably go to heaven
soon also. The poor women. Why had they suffered? They
had been kind to many people. That would count for a lot
in heaven, wouldn't it? If anyone should live in splendor in
eternity, it was these two.

I did the right thing in coming. I knew then. God did not
want them to be by themselves when my mother faced the end
on this earth. I could not believe God would want her in such
pain. I was my mother's angel, Aunty told me then. She and
I ate a bit of the food I had while my Mama slept. Soon we
joined her, the first good sleep I had since I heard about my
mother's suffering.

My father died long ago. My mother was long a widow.
Like my Aunty. No one bothered them, even though some
older women were raped by the soldiers. What evil causes
such a thing? Is heaven as good as earth is bad? I often
wondered that.

In the night I needed to relieve myself. I thought I should
pee in the bucket in the corner. But then I decided to go
outside. I wanted to see the stars over my village in the black
of night once again. Like I did many times as a child. It was
always like magic to me. My insides became full with joy and
peace all at once when I saw this beauty. It is not like that

in the big city of Kigali where I live now. The lights of the city make the stars dimmer. Yes, I wanted to see the stars over my old village one more time.

It was a mistake. As soon as I moved out the front door, the men grabbed me. They must have been waiting for me. They were afraid to enter the hut where my good mother lay dying, but not to grab me outside its door.

I will not tell you all they did to me. But you know what bad men do to women. And here they want to ruin women. They put sticks in your birthing place to tear your body. Then the poops run out where only babies should be born.

In the night, my mother died. I crawled back into the hut before she did. Aunty was roused from her sleep when my mother gasped her last death breaths. Aunty was so upset when Mama left us she didn't see what had happened to me.

The next day we buried my Mama. The funeral was not fancy. Not like big men of the village get. But we gave my mother the best we could that day. Villagers came and told me good, kind things she had done for them. None of them knew, including Aunty, that I was suffering from the rapes.

After the funeral, I wanted to leave right away. I was still weak, but I had to get out of that place. Aunty agreed to come with me. She was a widow by herself now. With my mother, the two were a team. Strong because of each other. But no more. Aunty was weak too and probably would not live long. But I could not leave her in that place to die alone.

I think she figured out at some point what happened to me. She was tender toward me. She realized what I had gone through to help my mother.

We crossed the border from Congo into Rwanda. Aunty was tired. I left her sitting under a tree and went to find my friend. He said he'd wait for me. He would help us. I trudged along in a daze to find him. I wondered in a tight heart if he would leave me when he found out what the men had done to me. If somehow we saved money again and the surgery would not work a second time. If he could not enjoy me as a man and woman do together.

There he is! For the first time in days, I felt joy in my heart when I saw his kind smile. Love for me shone in his eyes. As soon as he got near me, though, he smelled the flow of pee and poops the rape and tearing brought. I saw the flash of pain in his eyes. Immediately he understood what had happened.

Then he leaned over and kissed me tenderly. "Welcome back, my love," he said.

MOROCCO

WESTERN SAHARA

ALGERIA

TUNISIA

LIBYA

EGYPT

MAURITANIA

MALI

NIGER

CHAD

SUDAN

ERITREA

DJIBOUTI

SENEGAL

GAMBIA

GUINEA BISSAU

GUINEA

SIERRA LEONE

LIBERIA

BURKINA FASO

COTE D'IVOIRE

BENIN

TOGO

NIGERIA

CAMEROON

EQUATORIAL GUINEA

GABON

CONGO REPUBLIC

CABINDA

CENTRAL AFRICAN REPUBLIC

SOUTH SUDAN

ETHIOPIA

SOMALIA

DEMOCRATIC REPUBLIC OF THE CONGO

UGANDA

KENYA

RWANDA

BURUNDI

TANZANIA

COMOROS

ANGOLA

ZAMBIA

MALAWI

MOZAMBIQUE

MADAGASCAR

NAMIBIA

ZIMBABWE

BOTSWANA

SWAZILAND

LESOTHO

SOUTH AFRICA

GHANA

NORTH AFRICA

SUB-SAHARAN AFRICA

3

THREADS OF HOPE
IN GHANA

*"I was always looking miserable.
My friend would see me in the same cloth
every time. And she gave me half a piece
of cloth. I was happy, very happy. I could
change my one cloth to a new one!"*

Aunty Margaret, a destitute widow who wore
the same dress for six years

One of the first things a newcomer notices on the streets of ghana is all the colors. Ghanaians love to dress in bright African designs that radiate a well-deserved cultural pride. Their colorful garb stands in sharp contrast to the homogenous Western look that's crept into the cultural fabric of Africa. Women of Ghana – rich and poor, young and old – wear dresses fashioned from yards of brilliant-hued cloth to reflect a vibrant Ghanaian spirit. For many, smiles easily join the picture, perhaps because Ghana has escaped the wars that have embroiled numerous African countries in the recent past.

This West African nation knows what it is to overcome. It was the first place in Sub-Saharan Africa where Europeans traded in gold and slaves. But it was also was the first black African country to gain independence from a colonial power, in this case, Britain. Its name was then the Gold Coast. But the country's new leaders renamed it Ghana, an African word meaning "warrior king." The first president of free Ghana, Kwame Nkrumah, was a warrior king himself who championed freedom across Africa, until he died an untimely death in a coup. Countries battling over Africa's riches during the Cold War, including unfortunately my own, were rumored to have a hand in that.

Today, Ghana is still one of the world's largest producers of gold. It has also recently discovered huge off-shore reserves of oil. China is a large user of that oil, involving billions of dollars annually, and Mandarin Chinese is taught in Ghana's high schools and universities. Massive Akosombo Dam has created the largest manmade lake in the world and supplies hydroelectric power for many in the nation. When I visited the control building over the dam, it reminded me of something out of a James Bond movie due to its modernity, size, and sheer power.

Ghana is even engaging in space exploration and preparing to launch a satellite. But the reality on the ground is very different. Many roads are hard to travel. Millions of poor scramble for jobs. And everywhere you go, you see women (and some men) carrying goods of all types on their heads, from big pans of artfully arranged groundnuts (peanuts) to bags of water, to live snails. I once even saw a strong, stocky woman carrying a refrigerator on her head sideways! Many poor women come from the countryside to the cities to sell wares or simply work as porters carrying other people's loads. Many of them have nothing and end up sleeping in the open, raped and gang-raped. Shelter becomes an urgent need.

But perhaps the biggest load of all falls on widows. Ghana is one of the few African countries thus far to outlaw humiliating widowhood rites, but that has not eliminated their practice across the country, especially in the villages. Ghana has also outlawed property grabbing from widows, but that still happens too. And land disputes are many. In 2006, Ghana reportedly had 35,000 ongoing land conflicts of all types.[1] Though profoundly affected, widows tend to end up as very small players, if involved at all, in these many land battles.

As in the rest of Africa, religion plays a large role here. Reportedly, 71% of the population professes Christianity.[2] On Sunday mornings, Ghana vibrates with worship music blaring out from churches small and large as people flock to them. The hips of the women, many of whom have hourglass figures, sway naturally as they walk to church in their best Ghanaian garb.

A recent former president, John Kufuor, did much to preserve Ghana's traditional dress by proclaiming Fridays as "Ghana Dress Day." This resulted from his concern that professionals here, as across Sub-Saharan Africa, were turning to western dress. With his announcement, designers began making some of the most stunning African designs on the continent, for men and women alike.

To actually buy an item of clothing, you don't go into a store as in the West and find something that fits as well as possible. Rather, you go to the market where the Africans shop and select a piece of colorfully-patterned cloth. A "piece of cloth" is six yards of fabric, and it's found folded among stacks of many designs and colors. With those six yards, you can make a full-length dress for a woman and the ubiquitous wrap to go with it. Then you choose a style, or combination of styles, from a laminated poster with photos of different skirts, sleeves, etc. Then a tailor, perhaps one sitting in the market, takes your measurements and puts it all together. The final product fits to perfection.

A 'piece of cloth' is six yards of fabric, folded among stacks of many designs and colors.

A Ghanaian friend insisted on having two dresses made for me that I wore in meetings from Ghana's Parliament to humble places with widows. I was wearing one when I met Faustina, a young Ghanaian widow.

FAUSTINA

Faustina

Faustina has the most beautiful skin color I think I've ever seen, a glowing bronze that the world's top models would envy. Like many of Africa's widows, she is still relatively young, only 31, with small children, a boy of 5 and a girl of 8. Her husband had died at age 40 of a heart attack just four months before we spoke. As a widow in Africa, even such a young and lovely one, the chances she will ever remarry, especially with another man's children, are slim.

Faustina makes her meager living selling sandals from a basket. She spends most days weaving in and out of stopped cars on busy dirt roads, trying to sell the sandals to people in cars as they stop for traffic.

I met Faustina through the organization that had given her a modest "microloan" for her sandal-selling business. She made the equivalent of about one U.S. dollar on each pair of sandals, and that was all she and her two children had to live on. I still wonder how many she could sell on a good day. She was obviously intelligent, but this was the best living that was available to her.

Akosua, a professional woman with the microfinance agency that had given Faustina her loan, translated as Faustina told her story and choked back tears.

"One Saturday I was at the market when people called to tell me that my husband had a sudden sickness. They took him to the rich hospital. They put him on oxygen. But he couldn't make it. Early Sunday morning he died.

"When I came home, I phoned his family that he was no more.

"His family sent for me. When I got to my husband's village, they told me that the funeral rites were to be performed in two weeks.

"I really suffered during that time. The family did not help me with money for the funeral. I had to use my microloan for it, and my brother helped me to get another loan."

Funerals are important and expensive events in Ghana, indeed across all of Sub-Saharan Africa, and can cost thousands of dollars.[3] Traditionally, the husband's various relatives, especially any working abroad, pitch in to help with the expenses. But not all families can afford elaborate funerals. And for a poor widow whose in-laws abandon her, and who is under enormous pressure culturally to bury her husband properly, even the cost of a coffin can be devastating. That is why some microloan organizations now offer funeral insurance to their clients.

Faustina continued. "The family told me to go back home to Kasoa [near the capital of Accra], and they would come later. When they came, they told me to give them everything in my home, including the bed. They were going to take my TV, divider, refrigerator, couch, carpet, bedroom things, and my husband's clothes. They would only leave the cooking utensils.

"My husband and I also had a plot of land. I did not want to give it to them. So I went to the elders of my husband's family. Their decision was not in my favor. The

My husband and I had a plot of land. I did not want to give it to them.

57

elders told my husband's family to come for my possessions."

She paused for a while, obviously in emotional pain, to regain her composure. I asked how she met her husband, thinking that would be more pleasant for her.

"My husband and I were from the same village. The mother of my husband introduced us. My husband was a graphic designer. He was generous and kind. We lived in peace together."

After the funeral, her husband's mother, though, "was leading the push to take my things. I was so surprised. We were very close. I took her as my mother. Now she refuses to talk to me. She says I'm the cause of her son's death. My husband was her only son."

"After my husband's death, they also wanted the land. It was a plot of land my husband and I joined forces to buy. It is in both our names." It is uncommon in Ghana for land to be in both the husband and wife's name, so in this Faustina is fortunate, but certainly not in the clear from having her husband's family take all or part of the land.

"My husband's family went to see the land. It is here in Kasoa. They requested the papers. But right after my husband's death, I hid the papers. I gave them to my big brother. I will let all go but the land." With land, Faustina and her children could survive. They could build a place for shelter and grow their food.

"My husband's relatives told me they were coming at the end of last month to take the things from my home, but they did not come. If I do not give them the things, I am afraid they will kill me. They will use the black medicine." She seemed genuinely afraid. I was at a loss to address that with her, but before we parted I gave her the name and phone number of a man who might be able to help her with her land title issue. She was very grateful.

Another widow, Emelia, then brought her husband's funeral announcement papers to show me. She said that in 2003 she and her husband bought land and put it in her name, but she fell sick and did not register the land. (Across Sub-Saharan Africa, land is often not registered.) Now a pastor is claiming he owns that land. So Emelia went to him about it. Then she went to the chief, and his mother begged the pastor not to take the land from her. But the pastor, Emelia said, broke down the room she and her husband had built. She and her child are now living in a storage container.

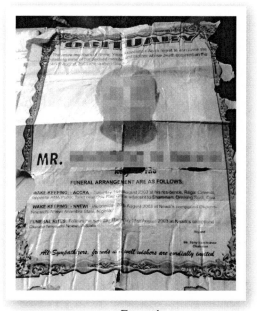

Funeral announcement

After we talked with a number of women individually, Akosua and I loaded up in our vehicle to leave. Suddenly we heard a shout from the second-story balcony of the office where we'd been meeting. A man said there was another widow. We agreed to meet with her.

The woman, Rebecca, came and without any hesitation sat in the back seat of the vehicle beside me. Widowed 13 years, Rebecca was a stocky trader of maize who travels to the hinterlands to buy her crop and then sell it in the city. She said she used to live in Accra with her husband and still lives in the house he built. After the husband's death, one of his brothers came for a share of their property, but she refused him, she said. Her son was 17 then, big enough to speak up and be heard, and he supported her in her claim.

When I asked if she had been afraid of black medicine, she laughed. "That man told me that if I did not give him a share then he would use black medicine to do something bad. I told him I was a Christian! I was not afraid of any black medicine!"

Rebecca's response prompted me to tell her about Faustina. I hoped she might be able to dissuade this young widow from fearing black medicine. But to my disappointment, Rebecca said she advises the younger women to give up things to the husband's mother.

"They are young," she said disdainfully, "and can start over. They can find another husband."

But Rebecca didn't have to do that. She had a home, a business, and an older son to care for her. What about the thousands of young widows left homeless and with little hope of finding a new husband with the children of another man? What about Faustina with small children and only sandals to sell? I also thought of a Ghana news report I'd heard about where a widow poisoned herself and her four children after her in-laws took everything she owned.[4] Rebecca was the only widow I met in Africa I did not like.

Until the older women had resources when their sons died, I realized, so they would not be so tempted to take from the younger women, the vicious cycle was not going to end. The ironic part is that since 1985 Ghana has had laws ensuring that in the absence of a will (currently rare in Africa) a widow gets a portion of her husband's assets. These laws, though, aren't known by most of the poor. Or the widows are intimidated with threats of black medicine, beatings, ostracism from their village community, and more.

Akosua told me she herself was shocked by what her fellow Ghanaian women were suffering. All the way back to the hotel, we talked in the vehicle about what could be done to help Faustina and others like her. We decided to suggest that the microfinance agency provide some information about property rights for women loan clients during their weekly meetings.

PROFESSIONALS WEIGH IN

FIDA is an association of women attorneys across Africa who volunteer their time to help destitute women.[5] The Executive Director of FIDA in Ghana, Jane H.A. Quaye, kindly took time to meet with me in her office, a second story walkup with fans blowing and linoleum-type floors. Their work in Ghana, she explained, includes educating women on their land rights. They go into communities, talk with the local chiefs and leaders, and train the women.

Land, she said, "is linked to so many things…food security, divorce, inheritance. And in many cases, women may have access to land but not own it." FIDA is trying to find ways to make Ghana's land law better, Jane said. Currently, without a will the law fragments the property among the widows and children in thirds and eighths. At least the widow and children get something, she said, a vast improvement over the husband's family taking all. First, though, the widow needs to know her rights. Then having them prevail can be quite a challenge.

Jane said that in northern Ghana, widow inheritance is a deep social practice. This is what was planned for my friend described at the beginning of this book if she returned to her home country. She would be inherited by the husband's family, just like the land and other possessions the widow had with the husband. If the widow refuses to agree, Jane said, she is thrown out. In Ghana too, even though it is outlawed, she may also be subjected to "widow cleansing," where the widow must have sex with a man to break the spiritual tie with her husband.

It is customary the wife is property, and 'Chattel cannot acquire chattel.'

Nationwide, Jane said, "The issue persists. Even though the law has passed, men still don't get it. It's customary that the wife is property, chattel. And 'chattel cannot acquire chattel,'" she said with disgust. There was that infamous phrase again.

But sometimes a male relative does not want the widow, and she and her children are just thrown out. "Most widows are poor," Jane said, "and often they are left to look after their kids with no source of support. They suffer from extreme poverty.

"Women are still suffering many injustices. We have good laws in Ghana, but the issue is how to get around the social/cultural practices that infringe on human rights. The African Protocol for Women's Human Rights addresses this issue but it is not taught. Various groups are doing bits and pieces here and there, but there is not a concerted effort for these women.

"Education is the key," she emphasized. "It is part of cultural practice that by ages 11 to 14, girls generally drop out of school. But, for change to occur, the girl child must be educated."

A Ghanaian pastor told me something similar. "Women should pursue education, develop themselves," said Reverend Dei Awuku, friend of a friend. "Women are taught to wait for someone to marry you. Women's God-given gifts are not developed. But if a woman is educated, she can support herself and the man treats her with more respect." Reverend Dei practices what he preaches. He told me he has put the ownership of his property in both his and his wife's names. I liked this man!

Bernice Aryeequaye, a rare woman who buys land and builds houses in Africa, came to lunch with Reverend Dei and me and explained that even civil servants like teachers and nurses cannot earn enough money to buy land. This brought home to me even more how difficult the situation is for widows.

Three more professional women confirmed the sad plight of widows in Ghana. Nana Oye Lithur, now Cabinet Minister for Gender for Ghana's government, told me over the phone that throughout Ghana, "the situation

They drive away the woman with empty hands, with nothing to eat, nowhere to sleep.

for widows is a big problem." The director of a women and development project, Patricia Fafa Formade, said many widows are cast off their land when the husband dies. "I know of many, many widows," she said, "who have lost their land, both Muslims and Christians."

A school principal (name withheld by request) told me, "In the villages they drive away the woman with empty hands, especially if she is not working. She doesn't know what to eat, where to sleep. Even with children, they will drive her away. Within a short time, she will die. If the woman doesn't have a place of abode, she will just kill herself."

AUNTY MARGARET

One brave widow who found a way to survive after she lost her home was "Aunty Margaret." I met her through a clerk at my hotel who told me she knew some widows who had struggled greatly after the deaths of their husbands. They turned out to be her aunts.

It was my last full day in Ghana, late afternoon, and I was tired after a long day of interviews. I'd bumped for hours over rough roads jammed with traffic and delays due to new road construction. My neck ached from one-too-many sudden bumps. It was hours past lunch, of which I'd had none. I half hoped the widows wouldn't show for our appointment. But they had been waiting for some time, the clerk told me, so I said I would meet them right away.

The clerk, a kind young woman, and I walked through a gentle rain from the hotel to meet her aunts at an old, empty office building nearby. I was wearing one of my dresses made in Ghana and had to lift the long skirt to avoid the mud and puddles from an earlier downpour. A freshness in the air after the rain lifted my spirits.

Two days before, I'd worn the same dress when visiting Ghana's Cabinet Minister for land, the Honorable Esther Obeng Dappah, at the grand halls of Ghana's Parliament. We talked about widows in her country's upcoming comprehensive land law, as we had months before at the United Nations when we met serendipitously there.

The clerk and I arrived at the old office building, abandoned now except for an old gentleman caretaker. The two aunts were sitting on very old chairs under the building's front entry overhang, waiting for us. The old caretaker for the building had let them sit there protected from the earlier rain.

I'd estimate the two aunts' ages as mid-to-late 40s, or even early 50s. They were not sisters by blood, but by the special kind of friendship forged by those who choose one another out of extended family relationships.

As Aunty Margaret began to speak, I studied her face. She had that certain beauty some African women have after age 40 or so, with high cheekbones and eyes of depth and wisdom. Aunty Margaret was very poor, but humble and dignified. She was also obviously intelligent and was proud to tell me she had gone through grade 4 of school as a young girl. She made sure I spelled the name of her tribe

Aunty Margaret

correctly when I wrote it down (withheld to protect her).

I'd heard widows' stories all day, but none was as moving as that of Aunty Margaret, who told me her story with depth and forthrightness. Seventeen years before, her husband had died and she was left with four children, including a baby. After the funeral, she went home to visit her family and then returned to the house she had shared with her husband, where, traditionally, his family was to care for her and her children. But that is not what happened.

When Margaret returned home, she found that another person was living there, and her husband's family, instead of caring for this widow and her children, had taken all her belongings. Her home was no more, already rented to someone else. For the next six years, she and her children were so poor that Margaret wore the same dress every day.

One child fell ill and there was no money to care for him, so he died. "Then there was three," she said. Here her composure faltered. Essie and I waited as she fought tears. When she recovered, more of her story poured out.

"The education was too hard for us," she continued, "and there was no help at all. I had to withdraw the older ones from school."

Before her husband died, his parents were nice to her. "It was after he was dead that they did not treat me well. It was for their benefit that they treated me that way. They don't care. They don't even want to see you. After they collect, they throw you off. They don't give you a *pesewa*." A *pesewa* is the lowest Ghanaian coin.

"The older women don't stop it," she continued. Some of them are wicked. You may be good for your husband while you were together. But after he is dead, the parents will tear you down. Because they will collect something from his benefit and job. They can use their doctor to go and sign and collect as the wife. They will collect and throw you away. "I got frustrated because there was no helping hand," she continued. "The children were crying for food. I don't have anywhere to get it for them. I was always miserable. I don't sleep in the night. I think where to get food for my children. I was so dry. I began to pray at night. I am Roman Catholic. I joined the meeting of Saint Theresa.

"Then a friend at church asked of my problem, because I was always looking miserable. She would see me in the same cloth every time. Because what I'm doing, you can't buy something out of it. I should use that to buy corn and ingredients to feed [my children]. She asked of my problem and I related my stories to her. And she gave me half a piece of cloth."

"I was happy, very happy. I could change my one cloth to a new one!" This was after six years of wearing the same dress. Half a piece of cloth would be three yards, enough to make another sleeveless long dress. She could use her old wrap with it. Even half of a standard piece of cloth, shared sacrificially by her friend, was such a blessing to this poor widow.

"Life is still very hard. My two daughters, ages 21 and 22, live at home with me. They are not married. We stay together. I go for daily work at the *chomba* [the market] to help somebody just to get feedy [food]."

"My last one is now in school. Daniel. He is very intelligent. He says, 'Mommy, help me to finish my school.' I say, 'I'll come and help you one day [with the school fees].' I weep every day [when I cannot help him].

"You can't even get anything to do as a job. I can read and write. But if you could get something like a job to do, you could use that to help your children. But there is no job. You can't get anything to do. Unless in the *chomba*. You work the booths, help to work, you get something to eat."

Then I asked her if she had told anyone else her story. "In Ghana you don't go to somebody to share your problems," she answered. "I know people who have lost their husbands, but I

Widows don't tell their stories. Who do you tell? Because here it's common.

don't know their problems. People don't tell their stories. Who do you tell? Because here it's common. It's very common. Even if you tell anybody, nobody will mind you. They won't mind you."

What could I say to Margaret? Her life's dreams had been shattered by her husband's family. She had lost a child, perhaps because of their lack of help. Life had dealt harshly with her, but she was still a woman of character and kindness. I was humbled to be with her. She'd mentioned her faith, so all I knew to do was to offer to pray with her, two women equal before our God. Immediately she extended her hands to hold mine.

As we prayed, a vivid picture came into mind of the day when Margaret had returned home with four small children, including a babe in arms, finding it was no longer her home and all her belongings had been taken by her in-laws. I could only imagine the shock and horror, the abandonment, the frantic moment of disbelief and searching for a way to make it not true.

Then something rose up in me. "God was with you that day," I said emphatically. "He was grieved and angry at what was happening to you." I felt the same way.

We both decided to forgive her husband's parents to lift that burden from our hearts, giving it to God to deal with. Then Margaret had an odd look and exclaimed that the pain in her arm was gone. I hadn't known she was in pain. She and Essie started whooping for joy. I was totally surprised and amazed. But if our God wanted to touch this widow's arm, who was I to question it?

Margaret smiled so radiantly in her joy then that I could see the beauty of her youth. Perhaps God had indeed met her in the sanctuary of the old lobby on the old chairs in the office building, giving her a new life, touched by supernatural grace instead of man's inhumanity to man.

Together, we walked happily out of the old building and breathed in the air made fresh by the afternoon rains. Then Aunty Margaret caught herself, saying she wanted to thank the old watchman who had let us sit under shelter. She might have been poor, but she had class. I was so impressed that she remembered the watchman. She called to him, a distance away, thanking him in a language I did not understand. He came right over to us, smiling a beautiful smile. He had the power that day whether we could sit under shelter, and he had generously shared his domain with us.

HEADING HOME

The next day on the flight home I sat next to a stylish and educated young Ghanaian woman who worked at Shell Oil. She told me about her aunt, who had also lost her home to her in-laws when widowed, even though she was an educated, sophisticated woman. Her niece added that people she knows have wills (in contrast to the poor who usually do not), but even among her friends, having life insurance is not considered a good idea, because superstitions come into play that such insurance may hasten death.

When my plane arrived late in New York, I had missed my connection, so the airline put me up in a hotel overnight. My taxi driver the next morning to the airport turned out to be from Ghana. He'd left many years before and still sent money back to relatives there, probably for funerals too. When I told him what I was working on, he stiffened in his driver's seat. "You can't change our culture," he said. "The wives need to get along with their mother-in-laws."

We were almost at my drop-off point. I didn't have time to tell him about Faustina, who had been very close to her husband's mother, only to have her turn on Faustina, or about Aunty Margaret, or others I'd spoken to. Or that the Ghanaian Parliament itself had passed a law to make their culture fairer to widows. I can only hope the full plight of widows will become better known to him and many others.

On my last flight home, I realized I would not have met Aunty Margaret at all, or heard about her "half a piece of cloth," if high winds hadn't cancelled my original flight to Ghana. Because of that, I had postponed the trip for a couple weeks, and the brand new hotel where I met Aunty Margaret's niece wouldn't have been opened yet. I wouldn't have met Aunty Margaret, who spoke so eloquently on behalf of Ghana's many desperate and courageous widows, giving this book its title. This was only one of multiple occasions where destiny seemed to play a hand in whom I met, so the African widows' stories could be told.

HALF A YAM

My baby is sick. Will I find enough seashells today to take my baby to the witch doctor for medicine? I know I have four other children, plus two more gone now from the sleeping sickness. Like their father. I was still carrying the baby within me then. But I cannot think about that. I must think about my baby, out of my body only a few weeks and sick like the others I lost.

I named her Precious for my favorite aunty who gave me secret little treats of the best foods when I was a girl. Usually the boys got the best. So we kept her treats to me a secret. She called me her "Precious" then. Now I have my baby Precious. Somehow I must help her.

Yes, I know it is dangerous for a woman to come to this beach alone. The men want this to be their beach, so only they can make money from it. Too many of them buy some drink selling big shells they find, so they can forget themselves, and their families. But I will not forget my Precious.

Here, look sharp! I must not let the sand and waves make my eyes lazy and miss what could save my baby. All day I have searched. I have found only this one little shell. Yes, it's pretty, but not enough, not enough for the witch doctor to even invite me into his hut. So I will trade it for half a yam for supper. That is all it will bring, but at least we will have that.

Maybe I could pray. Is there a God who made this shell? The witch doctor wants us not to talk about that God. But my aunty, the one who called me Precious, told me about her God.

Oh, God of my Aunty, please protect me as I walk home alone in the fading light. And please, would you come visit my little Precious tonight in our hut? It's humble, but if you are kind like my aunty who loved you was, I don't think you will mind. And we will sing for you — it is the only gift we have to offer. Please, heal my little baby so she can grow up to be as Precious to you as she is to me.

And please, help Mama Nana to be generous to me today in

return for this small shell.

"Aye, Little Mama," Mama Nana said when I reached her. "Found nothing more than this little shell today? It is nice, but so little."

"No, Mama Nana, this is all."

"Well, here is half a yam. It is good for you that the crop grew large this time. It will feed all your young ones a supper."

"Yes, Mama Nana, you are kind to give us a full half. I hope that your number of shells grows very large, larger than your biggest yams, so you can sell the shells for many pesewa. You should have good success because of your many kindnesses to me."

"Eh, it is hard to see you suffering so much since your man passed. And now with his last child sick too. He was a good one, and we do not have many of those in this village."

"You are right, Mama Nana. He was good."

At that, I could talk no more of my husband. It reminded me of my husband's older brother, who wanted to take me as his third wife. He is much older, and not good like my husband was. And oh, his first and second wives! They do not want this. They are older now too and have forgotten how to be kind. They do not want to share the land and huts and animals with my children. There would be much bad fighting with their children too. So I have told the man I must wait to heal more from birthing the baby. But that is just a reason to make him wait as long as I can. I do not want to marry him. I will pray and sing about that tonight too.

As I left Mama Nana, she warned me again about going to the beach alone. "It is not wise, Little Mama, even if your baby needs the medicine. Marry the man. He will take care of you!"

As I walked home, I wondered how much longer my husband's family will let me stay if I do not marry the oldest brother soon. At the hut, my children sang out in joy to see me. "Mama, you are home!" My oldest daughter, Nala, is always glad to see me. My second born, a son who now tries to

71

boss me and his sisters around, spoke up too. "Yes, we want to eat our supper! What do you have for us? Oh, yams. Well, at least it is a big half tonight." I was glad to hear his good heart in his last words.

Nala, only seven, had Precious on her lap, but the baby was sick and crying. At least she was still hungry. That meant the end was not close, like when a spitting cobra sinks its fangs into you and brings a quick death. The eyes of those in my village go wide with fear at the mention of those snakes. Well, I hated this sickness that was trying to take my Precious even more than those snakes.

After our supper, and feeding the baby milk from my body, I told the children that we were going to invite Aunty's God to come to our hut that night. Nala, her eyes wide in wonder, asked, "He would come, here, Mama?"

"We will see, my lovely one. Today at the beach, I asked him to come tonight and told him we would sing for him." I began by singing our favorite song, the funny one about the monkey in the tree that could never jump as far as the other monkeys. The young ones joined in with joy like monkeys jumping in their hearts. Then we sang the song about the stars we watched at night. This was my husband's favorite. He sang it to me so tenderly the first night we spent together after his father brought two goats and a rooster to my father to make me his wife.

When I finished singing, the children were asleep, including Precious. I lay myself down, pretending my husband was still there beside me. I felt a peace, something new. As I drifted off to sleep, I decided we would sing to Aunty's God the next night too.

4

VALOR IN UGANDA

"I was inherited this year...
There was no other way for me."

Margaret, a Ugandan widow

As I descended the steps of the plane onto the tarmac of Uganda's Entebbe airport, I felt an impulse to kiss the ground. At last I was back in Africa! Could this be the same person who was once afraid to venture here, afraid of sickness and danger? I smiled to myself, pleasantly surprised at the depth of my joy.

Today, Uganda is considered relatively peaceful, stable, and prosperous. The recent discovery of oil and gas in the western part of the country has also opened new economic possibilities. As in all countries in Sub-Saharan Africa, though, many still live in poverty. And fighting in the northern part of the country in one of Africa's longest-running civil wars (from the late 80s to a cease-fire in 2006) has left many widows.

I was here at the invitation of Deborah Oyella, the Ugandan attorney working for the United Nations whom I had met on a 45-minute African flight. Deborah offered to introduce me to people who would take me to meet widows in refugee camps in northern Uganda. Actually, these are called IDP camps, for

"Internally Displaced Persons," people who flee trouble in one part of their country to a safer part of it. Refugees go to another country, like those who ran from the genocide in Rwanda.

In Northern Uganda, two million people fled the brutal two decades of civil war. Tens of thousands more were killed or kidnapped.[1] At one time, as many as 65,000 people were packed into the IDP camps in Gulu district, where Deborah had invited me. At the peak of crowding, an estimated 1,000 people died daily from disease and harsh conditions.[2] The camps were about to be "decommissioned" when I visited. Only the most vulnerable were left in them, like widows who had no place to go or no one to take them if they did. Some still fear the return of Joseph Kony, the infamous rebel leader.

Kony and his "Lord's Resistance Army" were notorious for abducting children as child soldiers and slicing off the lips and ears of villagers to terrorize them. Kony is still at large as of this writing and has reportedly been seen in several neighboring countries, including the Congo. Like most effective rebel leaders, Kony exploited old societal resentments. In this case, they went back to colonial times, when British administrators left Uganda's northern tribes out of modernization.

Uganda has also been the site of a decades-long battle over women's rights. Laws aimed at granting women equal rights in marriage and divorce have repeatedly been quashed. Rita Aciro of the Uganda Women's Network faults the country's president, who has been in power for decades.[3] At this writing, Ugandan law says a widow should receive 25% of the husband's estate if he has no will. But in reality, widows are often denied even that much, and female children are cut out of their lawful inheritance.[4] One report says 11% of the adult female population over 15 in Uganda is widowed.[5] But given the high numbers of young people in any African country, the percentage of widows even 25 and older would undoubtedly be much higher. As a gender, women also suffer in that the beating of them by men is rampant, with a study of rural men finding that 70% of them considered wife beating justifiable in some circumstances.[6]

I had arranged to meet Deborah in Gulu in northern Uganda where the IDP camps were. She recommended I fly to Gulu rather than take the bumpy five-hour drive from the capital. So I booked a ticket for a four-seater plane flown by Mission Aviation Fellowship (MAF). Through a friend who wanted to be pilot with them, I knew they had a great reputation for good pilots and equipment.

Deborah worked in Gulu and would be my contact there. She recommended a hotel. I would stay there alone, without anyone I knew also there. I was concerned about that, but a few days later, I ran into an old friend I hadn't seen in months who often traveled to Africa. He said he knew about that hotel. A Ugandan general owned it and no one bothered guests there!

That settled things for me until two days before I was to leave home for Uganda. Deborah told me she had just been called to work in the capital, Kampala, for a while. She could not meet me in Gulu as planned. But she would arrange for someone to meet me at the Gulu airport.

The idea of traveling into Gulu alone had already stretched my sense of safety. And to go without knowing anyone there? I wondered if I should still go. But tickets were purchased, other appointments made, and the IDP camps would close year-end. I said a prayer for guidance. Then the thought came to me this trip would give me "a small taste" of what the widows experienced being continually alone. I packed my bags.

The day after I arrived in Uganda's capital, I ascended into the skies in a four-seater MAF plane from a small grass and dirt airfield. The scenery was mesmerizing, with swaths of grassy, emerald-green land, radiant in the sunny day and punctuated by winding rivers, lakes, and sporadic huts. Before I knew it, the 45-minute flight was over.

A Ugandan driver named Okello John (name changed to protect him) met me at the tiny Gulu airport. Deborah had arranged for him to meet me. He had been a driver for the U.N. in Gulu, but I still observed him closely for a while. In the end, John became an incredible asset for my time in Gulu. He was resourceful and wise and had his own amazing story to tell.

My hotel was only about a third full. Behind it, a group of tall, skinny teenage boys practiced marching with sticks as substitute guns. "They're training to be security guards in Iraq," a U.N. colleague of Deborah's later told me. "A lot of young men from here do that. There just aren't enough livelihoods to be found here."

In the night I was awakened, not by an intruder, but by the sounds of a heavy downpour of rain. Oh no, I thought. John and I had planned a two-hour drive to the IDP camp. He'd told me how bad the dirt roads were, especially now with recent rains. We wouldn't be able to go in the pouring rain. When I awakened again, it was morning and still raining hard. I was only in Gulu for two nights and one full day. If I couldn't go to the camp that day, I wouldn't be able to go at all. And the camps would close before I could return to Africa. But by 11 a.m. the rain had stopped. John said we could go. By the time we left, the sun was shining. It gleamed on the many mud puddles John would dodge left and right driving to the camp.

Before we left, I invited John to join me for lunch. Over our meal, he told me a story he said he doesn't often tell. If Deborah had been there, I wouldn't have heard it all. When John was twelve years old, he was abducted by the Lord's Resistance Army to be a child soldier.

His parents lived in a village and had sent him to live with an uncle in a small town to help protect him. John's uncle was a local leader, and one day a group of rebels came to his home while

They were all tied up to march one behind another. 'We're dead now,' he thought.

he was gone. The rebels took a total of seven boys from the home, including John, his brothers, and cousins. They were all tied up to march one behind the other, John in the lead. "We're dead now," he thought. When the boys arrived at a rebel camp, they were interrogated separately by a rebel leader, John first. All seven boys told the same story about the uncle's activities, so they were spared.

One day a boy in the camp tried to escape. The rebels caught him and cut him up in front of the other child soldiers. Six months later, John bravely decided he could not stay any longer. He too must try to escape. He succeeded, but when he reached home, his parents, like the rest of the village, were gone, having fled the rebels. Eventually, John made it to Gulu, where he still lived. "Evil was in that bush," he told me, "but God was there too, helping me to get away."

WIDOWS IN THE CAMPS

Deborah asked Annette Okwera, a young attorney in the Uganda Human Rights Commission in Gulu, if she would accompany me to the camp with John as our driver. (Most visitors don't rent a car to go into the African bush!) Annette was dynamic and energetic and would translate for the women in the camp, who did not speak English. She wore Western professional dress, with a skirt to the knees, but when we stopped to get some water just before arriving at the camp, she wrapped a long piece of African cloth around her waist that went almost to the ground. It would have been considered disrespectful in that culture to go in to the camp with her calves showing. I knew this and had worn a dark-colored linen skirt that came almost to my ankles.

John and Annette first set about finding the "LC," a member of the local council, to check in. John parked under a tree and before we knew it, the LC was upon us, correcting us for not stopping first to see him. Apologies and explanations were made, and all seemed well.

Annette told him why we were there: I wanted to speak to widows in the camp to hear their stories. Within five minutes, more than 15 widows gathered in a clearing next to us. As I approached the group, an older woman in colorful African dress and holding a baby, probably a grandchild, came dancing in toward the group. Ever ready to dance, and sensing an opportunity to bond with the group, I put my arm around her shoulder and entered in to her dance as we approached.

Some mats and a few chairs were brought. The weather was good and pleasant for us to sit outside. The women wore old but colorful African dress. Some wore African beads, and all were either barefoot or wearing rubber thongs. I was dismayed to see the LC also sit down in a chair off to the side with us. I preferred not to have men present. I knew the women would not open up as much. But I also knew I could not ask him to leave. This was his domain.

I'd never done such a large group interview of widows before. Annette and I had strategized a bit in the car on the way about how we would proceed, but we were both surprised at how many widows had shown up in such a short time. After introductory comments about why I was there, that I was writing a book about widows in Africa to hopefully get more help for them, I asked if they would tell me their stories. Also, would they allow me to write them in my book?

We began by going around the group and getting first names and ages. I told them my age too, considering that was only fair. It was helpful for me to hear ages, as women and men in poor countries often look older due to the hard life of war, sickness, or poverty.

There are certainly notable exceptions though.

I honored the oldest lady by asking if she would tell her story first. Annette translated. Then she was followed by the next oldest and after that, the others as they felt ready. Given the size of the group, each story was brief, but I was impressed with the widows' forthrightness, and their collected stories gave a great cross-section of the widows' different and common experiences.

Caroldia, 73: "My husband died in 1990. I had nine girls. Two died. And two sons. They no longer study. We have no school fees. I was my husband's only wife. After his death I remained on his land. No one disturbed me."

Dorothy, 70: "I am 10 years a widow. Eight children. Two were killed by rebels. The rest died except one child. My husband was sick. He died from natural causes. No one helped me. I was asked to leave my marital home. I was chased away by my in-laws. I went back to my father's land. My own family helped me. They gave me land. I had a co-wife. She died, leaving me with three children to care for."

Margaret, 41: "My husband died in 1999. We had a lot of trouble. The LRA killed my father and mother. I had children to look after, seven siblings in addition to my two children. There was no one to build me a hut. I was inherited this year [the cultural tradition where a husband's male relative marries the widow]. I have been 10 years single. I just accept it. There was no other way for me. It is my husband's brother. His wife left him. So I am his only wife. One of my children was stolen, a girl age 13. She went to be a house girl in the city. But the woman kept moving, disappearing." Annette, the human rights lawyer in addition to translating for me, then started speaking further to this widow, telling me afterwards she advised her to report this to the police.

Dorothy, 48: "My husband was killed by soldiers while I was in the camp. Now the government says to return to our village. My grandfather had given me land, but another clan chased me away. That clan is extending their boundary into my land. They stabbed me with a knife. I fought back. So I have been in and out of prison with my five children." Annette told me later she was shocked that this woman was required to take her children into prison with her. Annette told her about legal aid.

Teregina, 58: "My husband died and left me with nine children. My husband had gone to a funeral still alive and happy and then my in-laws brought him back dead. His brothers are now fighting me for the land. I don't have a door of my own. I make bricks for a living so my children can go to school." No decent jobs can be had without a school certificate. "The eldest dropped out because I failed to raise money. I have told my in-laws I will not leave the land. They have told me not to farm. There is much verbal abuse." Annette told her to go to the Office of the Human Rights Commissioner.

Helen, 54: "I married a non-Acholi [outside her tribe]. When my husband died, his family told me never to return. They took away the land I was on. I have four children. I struggled to pay the school fees of at least one. The first-born is working. The young ones are not." Annette suggested an organization called Invisible Children might help with school fees. A government school is nearby but a parent must still pay school fees.

Linna, 60: My dancing friend. "My husband died in 1972. He was a soldier. I had four children and one died. I was an orphan child when my mom died. [The culture says a child is an orphan if the father has died even if the mother is still living.] There was no land for me to get. When I came back home, I lived with my brother. Then the LRA killed him. He left three children. One died so I was left with two. I had no means

They are extending their boundary into my land and stabbed me. I fought back.

of a livelihood. I do small, small jobs to get something to eat."

We have three children. I also had to look after two children of my co-wife who died.

Agnes, 38: I liked her hair, which was styled in corn rows. She spoke some English and told her own story. "Thank you. My husband died in August 2000. We have three children. I also had to look after two children of my co-wife, who had died in 1996. She was my husband's second wife after me as the first. After my husband died, the brother to my husband killed someone. So the people of that person burned all the houses of people related to him, including mine. In that house, I had things to sell. These were for a small microloan I share with a group. All these things were burned. I still have to repay the loan. I am trying to rebuild the house by myself." She pointed to the burned hut nearby. "School fees for my son are the biggest problem. I myself studied, was a teacher, but could not get a job."

I suggested, I hope not too presumptuously as a non-African, that she start her own small school for the children in the camp whose parents could not afford regular school fees. I recommended she charge much less, but enough so she could send her own son to school. I'd heard about schools like this. She looked hesitant, said she would need books for the children. Annette suggested an organization called Save the Children might give her books. Agnes spoke to me afterwards, just before we were leaving, and with a light in her eyes said she would do it.

Balbina, 44: "My husband died five years ago. Soldiers killed him. I was in the camp. I had two children. When my husband died I came back to my marital home. I was told it was my own problem to educate the children. Then my brother died and I was also looking after his one child. I had no money to put the child in school. I have to dig [to plant food] by myself. It is hard to sustain the children, altogether three now. I have no money for school fees. My in-laws are OK. They do not disturb me."

Jeria, 55: "My husband died ten years ago. The LRA killed him. I was in the marital home. The brothers became very violent. They would stop me from farming. They took their cows into my farming area to eat the food I had grown. I came back to my family home. I had five children. One died. Two were abducted by the LRA. I never saw them again. So I was left with two. One was a girl who gave birth and left two children with me and went into another marriage. The fathers are not known. I'm stuck in the camp. My marital family and own brothers have refused me."

Martina, 48: "My husband died in April '09. I had one child. There were three co-wives, so with me he had four wives total. After 'big man' died, no one in his family looked after all the wives. There was a lot of conflict about land with the relatives. Each wife runs with her children. I have been operated on four times. So I have no strength to farm. I don't know what to do. I need a hut. If I can build a hut, I have a piece of land at my father's property. I live with my mother who is also a widow." When I asked the cost for materials to build the hut, she said 150,000 shillings, which is about $58 U.S. at this writing.

Magdalena, 63. The women objected when she said this age, saying she must be older. With her missing teeth and wrinkled skin, I silently agreed with them, but it was hard to know for sure. "My husband died in 1997. We had three children. We remained living on my husband's land with the children. There were two girls. One gave birth to four children. Another gave birth to two children. A relative is helping me to pay school fees, but he was arrested for allegedly burning a hut. He has five children and they are now in my hands also."

I had five children. Two were abducted by the LRA. I never saw them again.

Esther, 40: "In 2004 my husband died. I had five children. My husband and I had been taken in to the bush, abducted by rebels. The children were left in the house by themselves. I managed to escape after two days. He never came back. My brother brought me a report that my husband died. I was chased off the land. There was a lot of conflict. So I came back to my father's land with five children. The problem is paying school fees. You have to have the school papers to get a job, even if you know how to speak English and write."

Grace, 39. With a great tone and tempo to her voice: "My husband died in 1995. He had been taken by the LRA. We had been married two years. Other people in the village were taken too and escaped the next day. They told me my husband had been killed. We had one child. I was pregnant when he died. I stayed by myself and gave birth to the child. My husband was the only male child out of nine children. Now my husband's uncles say they want to inherit [marry] me. I refused them. I was supported by my husband's father. He said no one can inherit the wife of his only son, so I should go home. So the brothers to the old man beat him up because they said the bride price [paid for her when she married] was for the whole clan. So he wrote a letter to my father to come. It was not bad-heartedness, but he wanted to send back his daughter. My husband's father did not want to shame my father by sending me back. My father was a soldier. My mom had died. My mother's sister then invited me to live with her instead of being inherited. So I've been here ever since. I have one child in P-6 [Primary grade 6], one in P-4 [grade 4]. I am struggling to pay school fees."

After every woman had shared her story, I wanted to affirm them for taking the time to do so. I told them I hoped their stories would cause many people to want to help widows like them across Africa.

We said our thanks and goodbyes and loaded back up into John's vehicle. The local leader came over to the vehicle for his take, which Annette had forewarned me we would need to give. I handed Annette a modest amount she said was appropriate. But I didn't believe for a moment those widows would see any of that money.

Suddenly, as we were about to depart, one of the widows ran up to my window with a look of urgency on her face. "I didn't tell you the year my husband died!" she said quickly, Annette translating. Though that was not a critical fact for me, honoring her concern was. I pulled out my legal pad and turned to her name, Helen, and wrote her husband had died in March 2003. She seemed grateful and relieved that she too had told me this information, completing her story with the same level of detail the others had. I was happy to honor her and her story in that way.

As we drove back to Gulu town, Annette seemed fired up by hearing the widows' stories. As I've learned in interviews across Africa, even many of the local young professionals don't realize how hard life is for rural widows. Annette said she was considering taking some of her own salary to pay the relatively small amount (to a professional) needed for the one woman to build a hut. That was the story that had moved her most. To me, that woman could live with her widowed mother. Why wouldn't that work as it did in my country? But in Africa, Annette said, not having a "door of one's own" is a great humiliation. This is especially true for a widow who is already looked down on because she is unmarried. Annette then told me her mother was widowed too. No wonder Annette felt such empathy for the humiliated widow.

WIDOWS' ADVOCATES

The next morning I met with another gifted young Ugandan female lawyer, Gloria Ociba Nimungu, a friend of Deborah's. She worked at the Center for Reparation and Rehabilitation (CRR), a non-governmental legal-aid service provider run by lawyers and paralegals to work on land issues. Gloria was delightful – intelligent, a tasteful humility, just the right spark of strength when needed. She was a Senior Legal Officer for CRR, which was funded privately in Uganda and also by USAID.

Gloria explained that the center had mobile legal clinics to go to the grassroots level to hear individual land disputes, giving on-the-spot legal advice and/or mediation. The staff also trained people about their land and property rights, including those for women and children. In addition, her organization had a radio program that informed people about their rights, always a good tool in rural Africa where illiteracy is substantial. Women are 60% of the people they work with individually, Gloria said, and of these, most are widows or divorced women. The center also did some land negotiations and formalization of land agreements.

Gloria described a case that involved a widow. USAID was constructing storehouses for farmers for collective farming, and her group was helping with the agreement for the purchase of land for that. After four months of negotiations with the man they thought owned the land, a local villager told them the land was actually owned by a widow. Her brother-in-law had told the widow to shut up about being the owner, so he could benefit from the land sale instead of her. "You must be in the field to learn the truth," she said, "because land documentation is not good. When you're in the field, the truth will come out."

Traditionally, all of the land the widow lived on with her husband could be taken by his brothers after his death, whether they – or his widow – needed it or not. But according to Ugandan law, some of the land now belonged to the widow, if she filed certain paperwork and there were no objections from her children. Gloria's center helped the widow with the paperwork, and she became a beneficiary of the land sale. "She was very, very happy!" Gloria said with a smile. This widow was one of the fortunate ones. There were so many more like her who did not get such help.

Laws are in place, Gloria continued, to help protect widows, "but there is need for much sensitization," i.e., training, to inform these women of their rights. LCs, she said, will normally allow such sensitization of their people. "But some of the men in the villages will say, 'No, my daughters cannot own land.' Then some of the leaders will not administer the law in their cases, or the leaders are corrupt. They take bribes from the man so the land does not go to women. In many cases, women have rights over the land, but men say they're the owners, especially if widows are involved. Women are often denied their land rights. There is not an equal balance due to our patrilineal [male-oriented] society. It's worse in the rural areas where traditional justice mechanisms are used."

When Gloria's group goes to a village to do training about legal rights, she said, they always take both a man and a woman to speak. It's very important, she emphasized, for the village to see a man speaker supporting women's rights. Some of the villages, maybe 20-30% of them, she thought, have women on the local council. On average an LC has five leaders on the council, and if there are women, it will be one or two of them, she said. "More women are needed."

Then Gloria told me about "Principles and Practices," a breakthrough booklet that describes cultural protections for widows and was produced with the involvement of 18 chiefs and paramount chiefs. The booklet guides people brilliantly in how to follow the law in a way that protects widows but still respects cultural practices. I think it could be a model for all of Sub-Saharan Africa.[7]

"The villagers think the land act is so harsh," she explained. "But this book guides you on how to follow it with traditional practices too. Communities are beginning to see matters in a different light," she said. "If they are mistreating women, we explain to them, 'You're acting out of the law, and the law can take its course on you. The traditional practices that are supposed to protect widows are all here, too, codified [in the booklet]. If you're not following that, then it's not in your own interests.'"

It's important for the village to see a man speaker supporting women's rights.

I asked her what she thought needs to happen for widows in Africa. "Most projects for women address women in general," she said," and do not focus on the issues of widows. It would be great if a project were done just for the widows." As we were finishing up, I told Gloria I thought she would be a good member of Parliament someday. I told her I would remember her when she was an elected official! We smiled and said warm goodbyes.

Finally, it was time for Okello John to take me back to Gulu's small airport. Kindly, he stayed with me till the plane was ready for boarding. I was impressed when he told me he had made a will and left everything to his wife rather than his brothers. He told his brothers about this, and they were not happy. "But please take care of my children," John had said to his wife.

"No one wants to marry a woman with children," he told me. "If she remarries, she will need to leave the children with my family or hers and they will not have money from me to care for them. If she remarries, what I have left to her will go to her new husband. Culturally, the man controls the assets." I was amazed. How can a woman have any hope for new happiness with that cultural system, if she cannot maintain assets from a prior marriage for her and the children of that marriage?

WITCHDOCTOR'S WIDOW

The next morning back in Uganda's capital, Kampala, dawned grey with pouring rain. But my spirits were still good. I was looking forward to seeing the work of International Justice Mission (IJM) with widows here in Uganda, after visiting them in Rwanda. The plan was for me to go to the home of a widow client that morning with Florence Sitenda, who oversaw IJM's client aftercare. We talked comfortably in the vehicle on our way to meet the widow. Like so many Africans, Florence was warm and easy to be with. She was also a counseling psychologist and had been a school principal and university professor. She told me a bit about her personal life, that a niece who had been mistreated by a step-mother after her own mother died was currently living with her. In Africa, it seems, no one lives alone.

PHOTO: INTERNATIONAL JUSTICE MISSION

Eroni

The widow we were visiting, Eroni, looked to me like she was in her mid-30s, tall, slim, lithe, and joyful. I later learned she was 49. She bounded out of her dirt-floor home with great enthusiasm to meet us when we arrived and ushered us in to her simple home with wonderful fanfare.

There was only one chair in the small room and I started to sit on the floor, not wanting to elevate myself. But Eroni, who had just sat down on the floor, literally reached out with both hands and grabbed my bottom, ushering me into the chair right beside me! To say I was surprised understates it. Women where I come from, unless perhaps they are close friends, would never grab another's rear end like that! I looked quickly at Florence to see her reaction, but she acted like nothing inappropriate had happened (and to her culture it had not), so I did too. In fact, Eroni's bold and sweet action of hospitality endeared her to me even more.

Eroni could only say a few phrases in English, like, "I am very happy!" So Florence translated for us. As I always did, I asked Eroni if she would tell me her story, and if I could include it in a book I was writing. She might be poor, according to American standards, but her story belonged to her, and I would not presume upon that. She agreed, and her story began.

"I had a big problem. My children were deprived of their inheritance.

Another problem was the threats from my co-wife to kill me. There were two wives. I was the first wife.

"The co-wife took my late husband's property. Male friends were helping her with this because she had a lot of property and money from my late husband. There was a car, cows, land, houses, a number of rooms for rent. There was a commercial house with 28 rooms to rent. When my husband died, my children were not given a share. I have four daughters.

"One of my problems was I had only girl children. My husband wanted boys. So he took another wife. I was then driven out to this house. The house where I am now was built for one of my daughters. I was lucky to have a place to stay.

"Some people, a gentleman in the village I knew, referred me to IJM. They helped me a lot. They came and had a mediation meeting. They brought the two of us widows together. By the end we had an agreement to have my children get the rent from twelve of the rooms." IJM is now working on an arrangement to ensure the tenants pay.

"The co-wife made threats to kill me. I was so scared. Someone used to come at night, now and again, and bang on my door, push it. I discovered this person used to sit somewhere around the corner of my home. I found a sack with banana leaves, a machete, and some other stuff. I was scared these meant he would wrap my body in banana leaves.

"I ran to the local council leaders. They didn't know how to help me. I left home because I was scared and lived with a friend. I lived away from home for two months. I was grateful because IJM responded quickly. They called

The co-wife made threats to kill me. I was so scared. Someone used to come at night.

another family meeting with my co-wife, with other family. Alice [from IJM] was able to tell them the law against threats to anyone's life. Alice told my co-wife if anything happened to me she would be the first suspect. Then the threats stopped. If IJM hadn't helped, I think I would be dead."

Florence explained there are many people like Eroni, many who suffer like this. Generally, the local leaders help very little, she said. Widows usually cannot afford a lawyer, because it is very expensive. People also pay bribes to the local leaders and sometimes the police. Even women on the local council are few and basically powerless.

"My husband was a witchdoctor," Eroni said. "He had a shrine and patients would come. That was his job to get money. He got a lot. People would bring goats, chickens. I used to fear his witchcraft a lot. As a wife I was under his control."

After his death, she continued, "His witchdoctor things were sold by the co-wife. The shrine was removed. It was burned. The co-wife sold the portion of the land where the shrine was. The mother to the co-wife took it. She is practicing it now."

I asked Eroni, through Florence, if she were afraid of witchcraft now. Eroni picked up a leather Bible nearby and said she no longer fears anything. "Before, because my husband was a witchdoctor, I was inclined to that. But now," she said, "my weapon is in Jesus." Then she began to read the 23rd Psalm to me from the Bible in her language. When she was going through a very fearful time, she said, she read it six times a day.

IJM had also introduced Eroni to an organization that taught her how to make bead necklaces from long strips of paper she could sell. Eroni proudly showed me her Bead for Life identification paper and graciously placed on me a lovely long green necklace she'd made painstakingly, as well as a beautifully woven basket.

IJM was also helping Eroni with medical treatment for her children, then ages 10 to 17, had found sponsors for their school fees, and had helped Eroni with a poultry business. Eroni now had dreams of "making a big plantation, growing mushrooms and pigs." She hoped her daughters could study, get jobs, and be well.

"I have a new, overwhelming joy. IJM not only dealt with my property issues but they care. I am no longer poor. Even when I see people richer than me, I don't admire them because they don't have the joy I have!"

Before we left, Florence presented Eroni with a new blanket and some fabric for a new dress. Eroni held the fabric up to herself delightedly to show us and paraded around with it, saying she could wear it to church.

Eroni places a necklace she made on the author.

Then before we departed we had a joyful round of photos outside her home along with one of her daughters and some neighbors, another expression of community again.

TWO CHAMPIONS FOR WIDOWS

Ken Oketta swept into the lobby of my hotel in Uganda like a dynamo. I had heard he was doing groundbreaking work to redeem his culture for widows and Deborah Oyella had arranged for him to meet me. Ken is the "Prime Minister," like a CEO, he said, of the Acholi Cultural Institution. Eighteen ministers answer to him, and he deals with 54 cultural chiefs and one paramount chief for the Acholi people. The Acholi currently number a million people in northern Uganda, about 11% of the country's current population. When up to 65,000 people once resided in the IDP camps around Gulu, where I visited, most were Acholi.

Dealing with widows, and the land issues they face, is one of Ken's many responsibilities, but he has done so brilliantly. "Because the culture is broken," he told me rapidly, "life becomes survival of the fittest. Land is a resource the community needs. So widows and orphans become the victims of land grabbing. This has really escalated since the displacement of so many people during the conflict.

"Greed misinterprets culture," he said. "Or people hide under the cover of culture. They do this with gender-based violence too. Widows may come to their clan leader in the case of land disputes, but the clan leaders often decide for the man. But it is *cardinal*," he emphasized strongly, "in *every* clan in Acholi, to *protect* widows and orphans."

So Ken did something I've never heard of in any other African country. He gathered the Acholi cultural leaders together to document the cultural norms related to land, including those for orphans and widows. In the fashion of African culture, they met repeatedly and discussed together, as a group, what the culture actually called for. Then Ken documented what was agreed upon.

"We didn't write anything new," he pointed out. "We simply documented what used to be oral. Now nobody can be misled," he said. "We even define what a widow is." With various types of weddings, including civil, church, and traditional, this is important. The clear, well thought-out document, "Principles and Practices of Customary Tenure in Acholiland," states unequivocally that widows have the choice to stay on the land "to which they are married," or return home. If the widow chooses to stay, the clan should select someone to be a protector, and his role is "solely to protect the rights of the widow

They met repeatedly and discussed together what the culture actually called for.

and her children… [with] no rights over the land of the widow and children."[8]

Regarding being inherited, that is married, by a male relative of the dead husband, Ken says, "Culture demands we protect, not inherit, the widow. The protector should check on the widow, ask how she is doing in the mornings, check out any problems she may be having, like problem noises, bringing up the children. It is mainly being available to her, not necessarily financial support. The protection of the widow by the brother-in-law is *unequivocal*," he emphasized. "It is *demanded* by culture. If the brother-in-law is kind to her, the widow may want to marry him eventually, but she should not be forced."

He also said polygamy is not part of their culture. He doesn't know where it originated. "Polygamy relates to the anthropological dominance of man," he stated. "We should have the ability to control that dominance. It's a moral issue, not a cultural one."

This breakthrough document is now used by some legal aid groups, including the one I had just visited. They can now point not only to Ugandan law, which does protect widows, but also to the accurate portrayal of a healthy culture, as defined by the cultural leaders themselves. This brilliant solution is worthy of being followed by many African nations.

My last meeting in Uganda's capital was with Deborah Oyella, whom I met on that serendipitous 45-minute flight. Over lunch we talked like sisters, about life, work, family. She was warm, genuine, intelligent. I shared with her that I'd told many people about our incredible chance meeting on the plane. "So have I!" she replied, to our mutual delight.

I gave Deborah a small gift as a thank you for inviting me and setting up numerous appointments. It was a medal on a striped ribbon like an Olympic champion or a decorated soldier receives for valor. I told her she deserved it for all her work to help disadvantaged women and widows. It brought tears to her eyes. When we were done with our lunch, I was sad to see her go. We are still in touch, and I hope to remain lifelong friends.

INSIDE OUT

They've come in to the village! Is this a bad dream? I see it all by the light of my neighbor's burning hut! Or is it my hut?! No, this is no dream! They are taking young Kusizo! She has always been so slow. Now they sweep her along, a man at either side. They move her so quickly. She is going into a bad dream with them. So many in our village have helped her along when she was slow. But they are not helping her! I want to scream to her to run. But she cannot! I saw her eyes go wide for just a moment. Even Kusizo is not too slow to know these men are bad.

Their old soldier clothes have dark stains on them like from blood. Their eyes are liquid with evil. They have taken in the bad things that turn a man inside out so you don't know who he is anymore! What is happening???

I help old Nana, a widow. She took care of me when my mama died with the last baby. Mama screamed all night as the baby tried to come. Then she whimpered. Then she was gone. I could not believe it. Until now, that was the night of screams in my mind. My mama, gone. Old Nana came and rocked me like a baby while I cried and cried. Even though I was a big girl of eight. The same age as slow Kusizo is now. No one will rock her there while those big men hurt her. They had some boys with them too. Dressed in tattered soldier's uniforms with lots of stains. Their eyes were dull. They had seen too much evil already for their young eyes to hold.

When they came near Nana and me, she looked at them with such fire that they passed on, leaving me alone too because I was holding her, my arms wrapped around her to keep her standing. I have seen the look Nana gave them once before. It stood up in her eyes when a man in our village who was bad from chewing too many roots from the bush came by Nana's hut one day. All of nine years old, I was outside her front door with her, washing out our big old pot after supper.

He stumbled along and came up to Nana. "She is just an orphan," he said to Nana and looked at me. "Let me have her."

Nana's eyes flashed like hot daggers jumping from her eyes into that bad man. She said words to him I could not hear. But they caused him to jump back. After that, none of the men in the village bothered me again. They sure didn't bother Nana. She never told me what she said to that man, but we all knew Nana was not afraid to slip through the village at night. It was whispered afterwards no man could sleep in safety who bothered anyone Nana took under her wing.

That night as a girl I only heard Nana say, "She is no orphan. She has me!" Her words covered me for the rest of my life like the warm blanket I shared with Nana to sleep. And I slept very close to her that night.

Now I held her close to me, holding her up because she could no longer stand on her own. But her eyes worked just fine. The soldier cowered away. If I could still smile, I would have.

The screams from the women rose from all over the village now. Suddenly, Nana seemed to become weaker. Somehow I found the strength to lift her up and carry her away. She was trying hard to make her breaths. I had never seen her do this. I laid her as gently as I could on the smooth bank down near the river. As the water gurgled past us, I began to sing to her, to shut out the terrible sounds of the night, like she did to me when she held me the night my mother died.

But it was all too much for her heart. I think she gave her last strength for that fierce look to the soldier who passed by us. To save me once again. Soon she breathed her last. It felt like someone had hit my heart with a big strong stick with all their might. For me, this was the worst part of the night so far.

As I wept for Nana, I wondered about my son. He was off with some of our men to track a lion seen near our village. The men took a few of the younger boys, ages 10 and 11 or so like my son, to teach them how to hunt lion. My son felt honored and excited to go with them. But I worried myself almost sick. Now I was relieved he was gone for this horrible night. Would the men and my son be safe this night where they were?

The night wore on. The screams died down. How long had it been? Hours? Minutes? Women lay strewn all across our village, bleeding, some dead, some wishing they were. Then for me the worst of the night came. A friend's boy came running through our village. "They've taken the boys!" he cried out. "They've taken them!" He named them quickly. He said my son's name. No, he couldn't have. But yes, he did. I ran to him. I grabbed his shoulders with both my hands. "Did they take my son?" I asked, shaking him a bit to make sure I was getting the truth. I had always been kind to this good boy and didn't want to hurt him, but I had to know and couldn't stop myself.

Then he looked at me. He was only 10, but he knew what this meant to me. My son was my only son, my only child. And I was a widow. I would have no one now. He didn't know I had also lost my beloved Nana this night. As gently as he could, he said, "Yes, 'Mma,' they killed our men, including my own father, and I saw them grab your son with these eyes of mine."

I crumpled to the ground, wailing. Then I jumped right back up, knowing this might be the last chance I had to get information from this boy after our world had exploded tonight. Who knew what would happen now?

"Where?" I grabbed his shoulders again, unable to stop myself. "Where did they take my son?"

"I don't know!" He began to cry now. "They just said they were going to make them soldiers. But they are only boys like me. How can they do this?"

I could see water beading all over his young skin from running a long way. And he was still scared and hoping to find comfort. But I had none to give him then. His tears began to come like the flood waters of spring. My own tears rushed to join them. Wailing, I sank to the ground again. I squeezed my eyes shut, trying to make it all go away. But I could not.

WESTERN SAHARA

MOROCCO

TUNISIA

ALGERIA

LIBYA

EGYPT

MAURITANIA

MALI

NIGER

CHAD

SUDAN

ERITREA

DJIBOUTI

GAMBIA

SENEGAL

GUINEA BISSAU

GUINEA

BURKINA FASO

BENIN

TOGO

NIGERIA

SOUTH SUDAN

ETHIOPIA

SIERRA LEONE

COTE D'IVOIRE

GHANA

LIBERIA

CENTRAL AFRICAN REPUBLIC

CAMEROON

SOMALIA

EQUATORIAL GUINEA

GABON

CONGO REPUBLIC

DEMOCRATIC REPUBLIC OF THE CONGO

UGANDA

KENYA

RWANDA

BURUNDI

CABINDA

TANZANIA

COMOROS

ANGOLA

ZAMBIA

MALAWI

MADAGASCAR

ZIMBABWE

MOZAMBIQUE

NAMIBIA

BOTSWANA

SWAZILAND

LESOTHO

SOUTH AFRICA

NORTH AFRICA

SUB-SAHARAN AFRICA

5

HONOR IN A
SOUTH AFRICAN
TOWNSHIP

"They made me feel like I am a normal person. Now I always forget I am HIV positive. I don't feel like I have a disease in my blood."

Nomonde, a widow's daughter describing
a couple who helped her

From my friend's lovely hillside home near cape town, I could see the ocean in the distance, stately hills of green to the side, and off in the distance, a sea of small roofs jammed together in one of South Africa's infamous black townships. It was common for the townships to be placed in the midst of nice, white neighborhoods. The struggling poor of the townships lived packed together in shanties. For years they had no running water or paved roads, while the more well-to-do lived in modern homes.

This picture of drastic opposites reflects South Africa as a whole. Considered the superpower of Africa, it has the largest economy on the continent. Yet many South Africans remain extremely poor and unemployment is high, about 25%.[1] The country's population is about 80% black African, but it also has the largest communities of European, Asian, and racially mixed ancestry in Africa, with eleven official languages. South Africa has been called the cradle of civilization, with some of the oldest human fossil sites found by archeologists anywhere in the world. Yet recently, it has had some of the most restrictive living conditions for large swaths of human beings in the world. These restrictions have included *apartheid* – the separation of whites, blacks, and "coloureds" in inhumane ways, including lesser education.

Perhaps the country's wealth and strategic location have helped foster some of these contrasts. Historically, the "Cape of Good Hope" was the gateway to the riches of East Indies, and South Africa itself is rich with diamonds and gold and, at one time, slaves.

And how about women? South Africa's Constitution of 1994 enshrines gender equality, yet the country has one of the highest rape rates in the world. A recent survey states that an astonishing one in three women in Johannesburg, the country's largest city, say they have been raped *in the past year.*[2] A 2009 survey found *one in four* South African men admitted to raping someone.[3] Incidences of child and baby rape are also some of the highest in the world, due to a myth that sex with a virgin cleanses the body of illness. And even though South Africa has a high adult literacy rate for the continent, such attempts at "cleansing" are far too frequent. South Africa also has the second highest number of people with HIV/AIDS in the world, with one in seven of its citizens infected.[4] Polygamy is legal, and Jacob Zuma, the current president of the country, has recently taken his fourth simultaneous wife with public fanfare.[5] All four wives serve as "first ladies."

In the midst of all this, a stalwart group of South African women of various colors have battled for women's issues. A range of legislation has addressed women's issues, but the marginalization of poor women, says a publication by the South African government, "severely compromises progress."[6] As with other places in Africa, widows especially suffer.[7] I was to meet some of them in the black township I could see from my friend's home.

TOWNSHIP WIDOWS

"You can't go in there alone," my friend Maureen told me. I was white, after all. It was dangerous enough for blacks. So she introduced me to Cheri Swart, a pleasant 20-something white woman who did go in to the township alone. She took women from the township to doctor appointments, helped them get restraining orders on unruly men when needed, and assisted them in various ways.

The township, Masiphumelele, called "Masi" for short, is one of the smaller townships of the Western Cape—about 38,000 residents. "Most of the people have moved here from the rural parts of the Eastern Cape to look for work," Cheri said. "Many still have family in the Eastern Cape who they will try to support if they can find a job. Masi was officially adopted as part of Cape Town in 1992, so it is no longer an 'informal settlement.'"

More than half the residents, she said, live in shacks made of wooden pallets, plastic sheeting, cardboard cartons, dirt floors with a piece of old rubber-backed carpet, and corrugated tin roofs with stones on top to help keep them in place during the Cape storms. Many of the shacks are one or two rooms shared by families of five or six. The family rotates turns to sleep in the one bed. "Every square meter of land seems to be occupied," she shared. "If you are very lucky, you may find a corner somewhere not locally owned and for which you will not have to pay ground rent."

Cooking is with a camping gas stove or possibly electricity.

'You can't go in there alone,' my friend told me. It was dangerous enough for blacks.

Water is from a stand pipe. A community toilet is shared with many others – waiting in lines is a way of life in a township. Heating in the winter is necessary and the cheapest form is a paraffin heater, which puts out heat and moisture, contributing to the many respiratory health problems people in Masi suffer. Shacks are very close to each other. "A fire can spread at lightning speed and become a disaster for many," Cheri added.

If the family is lucky, she said, the mother will have some domestic work cleaning houses about three days a week. If there is a father in the house, he will generally have no permanent job, "so every day before 6 am, he walks to the big road junction outside the township where, with hundreds of others, he stands, hoping to be given a day's work by passing trades people." Unemployment is estimated at more than 60%, much higher than the country average. "Most people are hungry, most of the time."

The rate of HIV/AIDS in the township is high, about 23%, according to Cheri. Alcohol abuse and domestic violence, if men are present, are also high. Even Cheri didn't go in to the township at night. In the midst of this poor and dangerous township, like many across South Africa, widows and their children may suffer the worst.

After we passed many of the densely-packed shacks, Cheri drove up to a relatively nice block building in the township, a community center run by an NGO (non-governmental organization) where my first interviewee worked. Natalie greeted us warmly if somewhat self-consciously. She led us into a large room with no furniture except for a handful of plastic chairs. We pulled those up by a window for seating and light.

Natalie, then 41, was short with a happy, round face and pleasant manner. She worked with children at the NGO, which provides a safe place and after-school clubs where children can learn life skills. Her story began easily enough. Natalie was born in a small town in the Eastern Cape. She married and her husband was a paramedic. They had a son and she also had another son from a prior relationship. But her husband started getting sick, thinner and thinner. Then he died after a long sickness. "I felt hopeless when he died," she said. She was afraid of stigmatization for her and her child, so she got tested for HIV. Fortunately, the test came back negative.

"After a year," Natalie said, "another guy came. He proposed, and I jumped to it, too soon. We got married by the priest. We came here to this area. It was good at the beginning. But then he started to drink, abusing me and the kids verbally. One night he chased me and the kids out. The neighbors came to intervene and he let us back in. But every Friday, Saturday, and Sunday he would drink, and be abusive.

"Then this year . . . one time he went to the cupboard and got a knife. Fortunately a guy he works with came to my house and stopped him. I ran out and went to the police. I was bleeding. They told me to go to the magistrate and get a protection order. He did not appear at the court date."

"I took her to the police," Cheri said. "But a certain amount of violence here is accepted. There are some GBV (Gender-Based Violence) campaigns and helplines. But the man can beat his wife. The community has no say in that. The man says, 'This is my household, my family. I can do whatever I want.'

"Many of the women go to church," Cheri continued. "Many of the men don't. If a woman brings a pastor to her home to help, the man accuses her of being in love with her pastor. In fact, male church leaders do the same abusive things in their homes. I was at some workshops where even pastors asked, 'Why shouldn't I kick my wife?'"

Natalie resumed her story in a more serious vein. "Recently

my husband told the neighbors he would kill my son. I feel so threatened, not safe. He still has his things at my house. I think of moving out of this community. He has ruined my life. I am fearing for the life of my youngest son. My husband comes to the house and bangs loudly on the door until I let him in. My son, who is 12 now, asks me, 'Why do you let him in?' But I am afraid of what the neighbors will think if my husband keeps yelling."

I was alarmed by the profound personal shame keeping Natalie from protecting her son and herself. In my mind's eye I could envision a flimsy wooden shack door and an angry, vicious man pounding on it, till either it broke, or Natalie gave in. I also noticed one of Natalie's eyes had been injured. I wondered if her husband had done this, and Cheri later confirmed he had. Such a man might be capable of killing the son of the woman who had spurned and embarrassed him, the woman who had a court order turning him away. In a rage, perhaps he could kill a boy who was not his own flesh-and-blood son, but a reminder of another man who had been in his wife's life.

Urgently, I turned to Cheri as my host and asked if I could make some suggestions. Cheri quickly agreed. "Natalie," I said, "sometimes the greatest wound for a child is when the good parent doesn't stand up to the bad parent to protect them from harming that child. They know the bad parent is a problem, but when the good parent doesn't do anything about it, they have no one to trust. The good parent can then lose the child's respect and affection. This is especially true if the child is in fear of physical danger.

"Natalie, this fear is how your son must feel. And if you open the door to this man who wants to harm you and your son, your son will lose affection and respect for you. He will not be able to trust that you as an adult will protect him. You are a good woman, and you and your son deserve a good

He told the neighbors he would kill my son. I feel so threatened, not safe.

106

life. Please don't let this man hurt you both."

The three of us then proceeded to do some brainstorming together about steps Natalie could take to protect herself and her son, such as informing his school. I wrote down our list and handed it to Natalie. Cheri would be there to help Natalie with them. I also asked if there was a women's support group Natalie could go to. Cheri said there weren't things like this that she knew of in the township. In fact, one of her dreams was to start a women's center there with such groups. But we agreed to look for something for Natalie and see what could be done.

That night I was sleepless and troubled. Cheri told me the next morning she had felt the same way. She'd called Natalie before bed to see how she was doing. Thankfully, we would find some hope for Natalie with the widow we would visit the next day.

When we drove to that widow's home in Masi, I saw young men just standing on street corners as unemployment casualties. To me they looked lost, even while trying to make a show of being carefree. Loud music blared from various places.

Patricia (pronounced Patreecia) is one of those warm, happy people with a natural leadership gift. She met Cheri and me warmly when we drove up to her daycare in Masi for preschool children, called a "crèche." The atmosphere was joyful as about 25-30 children played outside on the dirt front yard. Patricia had not been expecting us, but she received us happily. I estimated her to be in her late 40s or early 50s.

Patricia

First she told me the name of the village she had come from, a common practice among Africans (withheld to protect her). Patricia was married at 18 years of age and her husband, who was from another village, was older, 25. They met on a school holiday. They had three children, two daughters and a son. They had their ups and downs, she said.

"Then he took me from his village to Cape Town, because his parents had moved from their village to the other side of Cape Town. My husband wasn't nice. There were beatings. When we would fight, he was hitting me in front of the children. You do things you don't like to do. He was drinking. All this drinking. You're not good any more. If you tell yourself you want to change, you run away. Then he asks forgiveness. I forgive him because he was my husband.

"Then he passed away from an accident. He wasn't sick [a needed disclaimer where so many die of HIV/AIDS]. He was shot. Someone was angry with him. He was in his village for holiday. My youngest daughter was three months then. Before he died, he was trying to change. He let me go to church, go to my friends. I start to say, thanks God, my husband is starting to change. Then he was taken away.

"My husband's death was a shock, very sad to me. I've got a baby. The policeman came to tell me. When he was killed, I was working for a lady and her family. She helped me a lot. I worked for them for many years. They were like my parents. They were such a blessing. Working with them I picked up experience with children. And they looked nice after my children and me. They bought me this plot of land. There was no house. I built that. Then they retired and went back to England. Without them I wouldn't have survived. I would have been angry.

"Every Wednesday," Patricia continued, "we have a women's group here. We share all our problems, like HIV, sickness. Maybe six or ten of us. It's a place to talk and share. We share everything. You mustn't keep things inside. We visit each other when sick. We meet about 6 pm. We pray, drink tea." Thinking of Natalie, Cheri and I asked if more women could come.

"Yes, we're open for more women to join. I know what it is like. I was thinking I'm alone." Cheri and I were thrilled to know there was a place where Natalie could come.

Patricia then enthusiastically showed Cheri and me around her crèche/home. I had to smile when she opened the door to another room. There lying on a narrow bed were about seven young children, all asleep on their tummies. They were so close I didn't see how they'd gotten to sleep without disturbing one another. But there they slept.

Also in the house were a small living room, bedroom, and kitchen. Patricia explained the smell of smoke was a result of a recent fire at her neighbor's home. It was so close I could have stood on Patricia's property and reached out and touched the wall of it. Patricia also showed us where the beams of her home had been singed. She was very grateful her home did not have more damage.

WIDOWS TOGETHER

Cheri told me the next widow we would meet had an amazing garden. That sparked a memory from my childhood in Georgia. When we drove downtown, we'd pass through a poor neighborhood. I was always amazed that in the midst of many run-down houses and properties, the yards of a few tiny homes were astonishingly beautiful with lush, green front yards and masses of flowers. It was a lesson to my young mind that poverty did not have to prevent one from creating nice surroundings. Some would break out of the mold and create beauty wherever they were.

The home of a lovely 44-year-old widow we'll call Niane (not her real name per her request) reminded me of that childhood experience. Niane lived in the more dangerous "spillover" area of the township with dirt roads. Somehow Niane had gotten a plot of land wider than most. Over at one side, in the midst of shanty building materials for the home and a front fence, was a stand of the biggest, lushest spinach I'd ever seen. It stretched the depth of the property and was probably about ten feet wide, with a fence along one side of it separating it from the rest of her property.

Niane was still lithe and lovely and moved with incredible grace. She later told me it was hard for her to sit still for long. So she focused her relentless energy on the garden, watering and nurturing it by hand. After photos by the garden, Niane invited Cheri and me into her home. I was surprised by its good size and how inviting it was. Two sofa loveseats faced each other, a coffee table was in between, and a chair sat at one end, all sat on a carpet-covered dirt floor. Sun poured in the open front door. Niane guided me to the chair of honor, placing her hands on my bottom to do so as the witchdoctor's widow had done in Uganda. This time I was used to it!

Three more women, friends of Niane's, appeared promptly as if by magic to tell their stories too, ranging in age from 29 to 44. Niane's 19-year-old daughter, Naledi (not her real name) quite a presence in her own right, also joined us and translated for the women in excellent English.

I noticed music played loudly in the background from across the dirt road, probably a constant fact of life in the township. But there was a sense of intimacy in Niane's living room, even with the music and the front door open. I was eager to hear the stories from these women and honored that once again African women were willing to take the time and emotional energy to share them with me.

Niane went first, but her daughter, Naledi, boldly started telling her story for her. Niane was 19 when she married. "She had gone to get water at the river. She was wearing traditional clothes of

110

a wraparound cloth around her hips and nothing on top. A guy saw her at the river and called to her. She ran away. He collected his father to go to her home. They tried negotiations with Niane's father. He said no. But her uncle advised for the marriage, saying if Niane got married first, as the oldest, then all would marry. So they forced her to marry.

She went to the river to get water and climbed a tree in her special dress to get away.

"It was hard. They bought new clothes for her like a bride. But she went to the river to get water and climbed a tree in her special dress to get away. But they came for her. They beat her and beat her. Another time, after she was married, she ran a distance, across lots of rivers to her house. But they came and took her again. She didn't want to marry. Her father didn't want her to marry either. She wanted her father to say 'Stay,' but he didn't.

"Her husband beat her a lot. If he was drunk, he would be angry and beat her." One time when Niane was cooking, he started beating her. But this time, Naledi said she and her brother, who were then about 10 and 12, took some iron rods and hit their father. "He never beat our mother again." Naledi said she vowed she would not live like that when she grew up.

"Mama was working. That paid bus fare for my father to get to work. Mama would ask him for money for clothes, but he said no." They told their mother they had to move. A woman from the U.S. was sponsoring Naledi for school fees (through a Baptist church and kids club). Naledi told the sponsor the story of what was happening with her mother. "The lady said you must look for another place and said she would help us."

Then their father wanted forgiveness. But Naledi told her mother she would move if her mother took him back in. "He had a big knife. We found out a woman told him he must come and kill his wife and daughter. Then he became sick. His tongue was shortening. He was getting mad. Niane took him to the hospital where he died. "It was easier after he died," Naledi said. "He never wanted anyone to visit us, even a cousin."

Naledi called it an "old fashioned" marriage. "It's where the man thinks he has the right to beat his wife. And the man always says he is innocent! The new fashion in marriage," this 19-year-old said, "is 50-50. And if your husband beats you, he must go to jail. Then you must divorce him, because he will never change." Unfortunately, that had been her experience with her father.

Next Serena (not her real name), age 36, spoke, with Naledi translating for her also. Serena was married in 1989. "It was a traditional marriage with no ceremony. The first year my husband lost his job. While he was not working, he was drinking a lot. He beat people when drunk, even the people he drank with. When I would stop him from beating people, he beat me. I had a baby, a girl, and my family in the Eastern Cape supported us. Neither of us was working. I stayed with my husband but he was still fighting. We had another baby. But it was never good anymore. I got three children from him, but nothing good.

"He used to put a big knife under the pillow, to scare me. He spoke terrible things to me. Then one day he went after me with a spear when I had a baby on my back. He threw the spear and it went right by my baby. So I left and went to another town. I reported this to his family and they tied him with a rope and beat him. I went looking for a job. I told myself I was not coming back to him. But he always came where I worked. He wanted to beat me there.

He used to put a big knife under the pillow, to scare me. He spoke terrible things to me.

"In 2000 I came to Cape Town. I stayed, selling fruits and vegetables. In 2004 my husband passed away. I received a call from his family. I don't know how he died. I felt nothing when he passed away.

"Family from his side came and negotiated with my family. Then they took me," in the common pattern of the man's family "inheriting" the widow. "The man who took me was living in Johannesburg and his sisters were my friends." She stopped talking and did not explain what happened with that man. She seemed vulnerable emotionally then and I did not ask.

Then she said with some pride, "I was 14 years old when I was married. Lots of people wanted to take me. . . My children go to school!"

But she still seemed sad. Her emotion and damaged self-worth, uncovered by the telling of her story, hung in the room like a damp fog. There was no way I could go on without a response. So I told her the terrible things her husband had told her about herself were lies from the pit of hell. I asked the other women, her friends, to share with her what they liked about her. They immediately rose to the occasion and said lovely things in a genuine way, like she was loyal, she never gossiped about them, they could trust her to keep things private when they told her personal things. An emotional warmth began to fill the room instead of the heavy fog.

It turned out she'd only told one person in the room her story before, because women in Africa don't usually tell their stories due to shame and so many people struggling with similar things. But now more women knew her story and still loved and accepted her. I hope some important healing took place for her that day.

Then, thinking of Natalie, I asked Niane and the others, "What would you do if you heard sounds coming from a neighbor's and thought a man was beating a woman there?" After Naledi translated, Niane sat up with a certain fierceness and said she would call the police.

"Every Friday we call the police on our neighbor. The last time they were helpful. They beat the man. They took the woman home to another place. Helped her take her stuff. She was screaming." Obviously Niane did not live under the stronghold of shame and blame that seems to incapacitate far too many others. Meeting her and her friends was quite an experience.

From there Cheri drove me to a small, pleasant property and dwellings in Masi with a tasteful wooden sign saying "All Nations" on one of the small buildings. All Nations was founded by a gutsy white missionary named Floyd McClung who moved to South Africa to train young men and women to become good leaders. Previously he and his family had lived on the drug trail in Afghanistan and in Amsterdam's red light district, helping desperate people.

I felt a sense of peace just walking on the property. Cheri and I went into a small wooden dwelling consisting of one room well-built of pleasing raw wood, with windows on three sides. There, I learned, groups of various ages and genders met to find some peace, to grow in their faith and life skills.

Several widows who did not know each other soon arrived and sat in a circle to tell me their stories. The first, Zoleka, was beautifully dressed in a skirt and headdress of African theme with an interesting bead necklace to match. Age 57, she had a grace and dignity only age can bring to some. She worked at a "crèche," another children's nursery, at her church.

"In 2007 my husband died of a heart attack," she began. "He was a nice guy who loved our five children and six grandchildren. We were married for 34 years, since I was 19 years old. One day I was listening to the radio. He asked me to turn on the TV. He was struggling. I put him with a big pillow. Then he was gone.

"After he died, life changed. At first his family did not admit me to their home. They called, telling me I've killed their brother. I didn't speak anything when they said that. I decided to make a video of my husband's funeral in the Eastern Cape so my children could hear all the speakers and what they said. Even now his family is not phoning me.

I don't understand why our culture blames the wife. Widows are blamed almost always.

"My husband was the eldest in his family. We have property from my husband's family. We stayed there for a long time. It is still my property. My husband's family did not take it. The neighbors watch it. No one is living there. This December I will go back for a short time."

"Many things inside the home we shared are mine, because I worked for a long time. It was a big shock that my husband died, to his family too. That's why they said I killed him. I don't understand why our culture blames the wife. If a woman dies first, they say nothing. Widows are blamed almost all the time. No one is close to you to console you. They are cross with you."

"It is no stress that his family doesn't speak to me," she said, "because I have done nothing wrong. But I've decided inside me I want my own property to give to my children. I will find another place for their safety. I want to be with my children and live with my own family. I will buy another place with my earnings. Because of our culture, I will not stay by my husband's family. I won't visit. I don't want anyone to bother me." She paused with sadness. "The relationship with his family was so good, so tight."

Then Princess, age 54 with a cheery face and smile, began her story. She works at a humanitarian organization. "I lost my husband recently. We were married for 36 years, since I was 17. We had eight children and six grandchildren. My husband was working in a mine in Johannesburg. Then he lost his job. He was healthy then. We came to Cape Town in 2001 and he was doing temporary jobs. In 2004 he got sick. He stayed at home sick for five years and the clinic gave him medicine. When he died, his family treated me so badly." Then she broke and wept. One of the other women got up to close the front door of the little room so she would have some privacy.

She composed herself and continued. "My husband's sister prepared the funeral. We were doing it together. After the funeral, his family started doing bad things. I was close to them before, but then they treated me badly. My husband and I had planned to live in a government house. But because of his family we could not live in that. Now I stay in a shack with 10 people total. We have no water, no bathroom. We use the toilet from the neighbor. But now my neighbor doesn't want the children to go inside to use the toilet. They throw them out." She wept again, understandably, at this humiliation in addition to her recent widowhood and grief. I thanked her for telling her story for this book, so it might help other widows. I hoped that might give her some dignity and comfort.

JUSTICE DOLL

The last widow I met in Masi, along with her daughter, touched me deeply. It was an honor to meet them. A friend of Cheri's, Joylynn Landshut, took me to see mother and daughter Nomendo and Nomonde. We drove up to a group of small dwellings with a narrow walkway running between them perpendicular to the road. The dwellings shared walls, and I was told a school was at the back. Music played from one of the small shacks, meaning everyone around heard it.

Nomendo and Nomonde were expecting us. As we came in to their small living room, my first impression was of order, cleanliness, and pleasantness. The room was filled by a small sofa, a refrigerator, and a card table with two chairs. Here the daughter, Nomonde, who was 32, and a friend made "Justice Dolls." These were an idea Joylynn had to publicize the slavery of women and provide a modest living for Nomonde and her family when the dolls were sold. One sits by my desk now. Brown wooden arms, legs, and head. Dress and headdress of colorful yellow, black, and red African print. Colorful beads around her neck. And her hands tied in front with black beads and a sign hanging from them saying, "Set me FREE." An accompanying card says:

"This is a doll with purpose. Her name is Justice. She reminds us that a victim of human trafficking (modern-day slavery) isn't just a statistic, but someone's daughter, wife, sister, or mother. Together, we can set Justice FREE .... Making this doll provides income for women affected by HIV/AIDS."

Mother and daughter welcomed us warmly. Joylynn told Nomonde there was a new order for a large number of dolls, 1,000 as I recall. I was amazed an order for so many dolls could be made on a card table in that small room. Once Joylynn and Nomonde had finished their business, we moved over by the little sofa to join Nomonde's mother, Nomendo, and begin our interview. The daughter translated for the mother, adding further information and explanations to help fill out the story.

The mother, a lovely woman with a kind countenance, was born in 1952. She had her firstborn at age 22 and then four children altogether. "They were in love," Nomonde said. Her father was much older. There was 20 years difference. They met in the village. His name was Mabandla.

"There were difficult times. He was not working. It made him

Nomonde and Nomendo

drink too much. My mother wanted him to look for work. Then he shouted too much. He found a job but went blind. I don't know why. He stopped working. He got paid for his blindness. My mother worked, keeping children, sometimes washing."

Nomonde making Justice Dolls

Then Nomonde translated for her mother. "Because my husband was blind, he was frustrated, angry, shouting. He wanted to hit me, but he never did. I told the family not to be angry with him. He didn't know why he was doing this." I was impressed with the mother's ability to show grace and forgive.

Then Mabandla passed away in 2001. I asked if his family took away the family home. Nomonde, the daughter, suddenly burst into tears and leaned against her mother's shoulder as she sat next to her on the small sofa.

"Yes!" she exclaimed. "They kicked us out!" The words came out painfully. Her mother looked at me, forlorn. She did not know what was being said in English and could see her daughter's pain. As a loving mother it was certainly not the first time, I'm sure, she had shouldered her daughter's grief, but she did not know what was happening. I tried to look compassionately at both of them.

Then something rose up in me. "I came here to tell your story," I said, "and many others like them, because this happens to so many women all across Africa. I believe God has seen your pain, and he is not happy with this. He

'They kicked us out!' The words came out painfully. Her mother looked forlorn.

wants something to be done. He wants many people to know and help. He wants things to change! I have traveled to Africa alone multiple times, even with my arm in a sling, to tell stories like yours. Thank you for telling me your story."

Strengthened by my response, Nomonde continued what was obviously now a family story, not only the story of her mother, the widow. The daughter spoke painfully, but eagerly, purging herself of the awful memories, of the terrible time just after they were kicked out of their long-time family home.

"They said my mom doesn't have a boy, so it will be a man who will look after my Dad's stuff, not a woman," she said indignantly. "We said we are not married. We need to stay in the house. They said no. They kicked us out. My Dad's brother kicked us out. One of them was bad all the time. Three cousins of mine were living with us. They were boys. Two were drinking. They shouted at my mom. She was just helping the children.

"My big sister had a little shack in the town where she worked. A man with a car near our family home took our stuff there for us and we stayed there. I prayed for getting a place here. I didn't want my father's family to disturb our sister."

Then I asked, "Do you know other widows who were made to leave also?"

The mom replied through the daughter, "Yes, I know another from my village."

Then the daughter continued with more strength, "We have a better life here than we had where we lived with our father." So Nomonde realized that being kicked off the land was actually part of their finding a better life. I said to the mother, asking the daughter to translate, "You have a very fine daughter." The mother smiled.

"Have you told anyone else about being kicked off your land?" I asked. "No," Nomende replied, to my amazement once again.

"Is there anything else you want to say?" I asked. Then she expressed great gratitude to Joylynn and her husband, David, who had helped Nomendo and Nomonde build their small home. Joylynn had also helped them find a living by conceiving of the Justice Dolls and selling them.

"I had a dream before," the daughter said. "Before I met Joylynn and David, I saw two white birds coming and a big sea. I was lying in the green grass and the two birds were coming. I didn't see which side they came from. I opened my arms. One sat on each of my hands. One carried a white book. I liked both of them. They put the book in my hand and left. I read the book. I kept it. I kept reading it. The book was telling me what to do in life."

"I liked this dream so much. I wanted to dream it again. Then I met Joylynn. In my life I told myself Joylynn and David were those birds. Joylynn gave me my first Bible. They are in my heart. They are in my dreams. They are in my life. I love them because I dream about them."

I turned to glance at Joylynn. "I never heard this dream before," she said with tears in her eyes. What a lovely affirmation that must have been for Joylynn, for the unselfish work she did day after day in the township helping people like this mother and daughter.

"They made me feel like I am a normal person," Nomonde added. "Now I always forget I am HIV positive. I don't feel like I have a disease in my blood."

This was news to me, but in line, I see now, with the mission of the Justice Dolls being made by those with HIV/AIDS. If Nomonde hadn't had such a glow on her face right then, with a lovely countenance and rich smile, I would have felt terribly grieved to learn such news about this special new friend.

Nomonde continued, "Before, it was miserable because I was in a place I cannot explain." Joylynn told me later that when she'd met Nomonde, she had been lying down, curled up in a ball, beaten down by life.

At this point, Nomonde's energetic daughter of about twelve rushed in the door from school, trying to interrupt and ask her mother something. Like all good mothers everywhere, Nomonde immediately corrected her daughter for interrupting abruptly about a trivial matter. She's not weak now, I thought. I felt honored being with someone like her and humbled by her goodness in the midst of life's trials, in this township packed with human suffering.

A few months after my visit, fire tore through Masi township.

DANCING WITH MY FATHER

I am flying through the air! How can this be? I feel such joy in my heart, in my whole being! I have never felt this light! This strong!

Nothing weighs me down . . . no bad things in my blood, no looks from the neighbors, no heavy bags in my heart. I am free!

Now I am dancing with my father! He is the father I always wanted him to be. He takes care of me. He delights in me. I know he wants me to be his daughter. I think I will explode with joy!

Now he dances with my mother. She is here too? My mother looks young again. I did not know she was so beautiful. Her smile of happiness washes through me like splashes of cool, clean water on a hot day.

I am flying again. But I am not alone. A man full of light is flying with me. He turns and smiles at me. I think I will burst for joy!

Now I look down and see my cousin. He is the one who took my body when I was 13. It was only two nights after my father died. He said I was an orphan now. No one would care. He was my father's nephew. I belonged to his family.

I wept and hurt. I thought I could not carry two such heavy bags in my heart. The death of my father and the thing my cousin did to me.

Then that cousin came to visit my mother and me at the township. After my mother was asleep, he did it again. I fought as hard as I could, but he was so much stronger. He had grown good strength in the village where we lived.

I know he was the one to give me the disease. I do not want to even say the name. To let the name slip inside me too like the bad disease that has gone into my blood.

But I see him now down below me as I fly over. His hands are tied behind his back. He has been caught for a crime. His head is moving around as he yells loudly and complains. He fights against the ties on his hands. Like I fought when he took me.

I know he will not escape now. Sorrow surprises me when it slips into my heart. Is this the forgiveness toward him I have prayed for? That I can feel sad when he is suffering? He had a bad father. He learned to be like that man. What would he have been like if he had a good father? Like the one I just danced with? I feel a package being untied from my heart. I feel even lighter, more full of joy, if that is possible.

Now I hear a child crying. I stir. That is the sick baby next door. I know I have been dreaming. But, a miracle too, perhaps. I feel lighter, more joyful. I rise to face this day. I will go help with the sick baby as soon as I have finished my work for today.

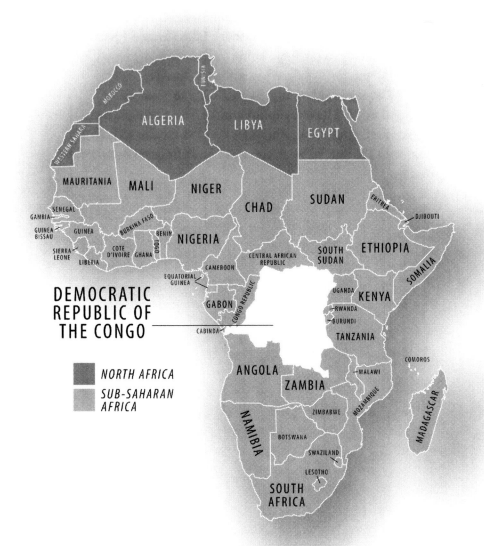

DEMOCRATIC
REPUBLIC OF
THE CONGO

NORTH AFRICA

SUB-SAHARAN
AFRICA

MOROCCO

WESTERN SAHARA

ALGERIA

TUNISIA

LIBYA

EGYPT

MAURITANIA

MALI

NIGER

CHAD

SUDAN

ERITREA

DJIBOUTI

GAMBIA

SENEGAL

GUINEA
BISSAU

GUINEA

BURKINA FASO

BENIN

TOGO

NIGERIA

SIERRA
LEONE

COTE
D'IVOIRE

GHANA

LIBERIA

CENTRAL AFRICAN
REPUBLIC

SOUTH
SUDAN

ETHIOPIA

SOMALIA

EQUATORIAL
GUINEA

CAMEROON

GABON

CONGO REPUBLIC

CABINDA

UGANDA

RWANDA

BURUNDI

KENYA

TANZANIA

ANGOLA

ZAMBIA

MALAWI

COMOROS

ZIMBABWE

MOZAMBIQUE

MADAGASCAR

NAMIBIA

BOTSWANA

SWAZILAND

LESOTHO

SOUTH
AFRICA

6

RICHES IN THE CONGO

"As you did for the Israelites, God, do for us!"

A Congolese widow praying for freedom from oppression

I said I'd never go to the Congo. For years I'd heard horror stories about the place. The most unstable country in Sub-Saharan Africa. The rape capital of the world. A country still bloodied by decades of fighting. I decided I would mention the Democratic Republic of the Congo in this book, but that was all. *No way would I visit it!*

That is, until I met a man on an elevator in Cape Town. From the badges each of us wore, I could tell we were both attending the same large conference. I was talking with someone else about this book. As soon as the man could enter our conversation politely he said with urgency, "You *must* tell the story of the widows in the Congo!" His words went like an arrow into my heart. I got his business card. He told me his organization assisted traumatized women in the Congo. After pocketing the card, I tried to forget about his plea. But I couldn't.

Back home, I noticed a Pulitzer Prize-winning play about the Congo was running. I decided to go. *Ruined* told of the war and rapes, but it was amazingly uplifting, showing the resilience of the human spirit. After that I heard through mutual friends about a woman named Katie Nienow, who was going to the Congo for her work with a U.S. microloan agency. I contacted her and she agreed to let me go with her.

The Congo has one of the most fascinating – and brutal – histories in all of Africa. The second largest country in Africa, it sits in the center of the continent, therefore its moniker, "the heart of Africa." The country's formal name is the Democratic Republic of the Congo, but it's often called DR Congo, DRC, or just the Congo. It's had other names too according to the whims of various colonizers and rulers… Kingdom of Kongo, Belgian Congo, and Zaire. A small neighboring country calls itself the "Republic of the Congo." But when people say just Congo, they usually mean the DRC.

In the late 1800s, King Leopold of Belgium had claimed the Congo as his personal possession. He was reportedly responsible for horrible atrocities. Congolese were enslaved in chain gangs to extract highly coveted ivory and rubber and an estimated 10 million died.[1] Leopold's selfish legacy was carried forth by Congo's president of 32 years, Mobutu Sese Seko, called "the Leopard." He is said to have bilked the Congo of billions, leaving it in shambles when he died in 1997.[2]

The next year "Africa's World War" began in the Congo, lasting till 2003. Sporadic fighting in some places has continued since. Eight surrounding countries fell into the "World War." It was the largest conflict in the world at the time and largely neglected by it.[3] Experts estimate that up to 4 million people died from killing and disease caused by the war.[4] Another 2 million reportedly fled their homes to escape the conflict areas. But fighting came even into the Congo's capital, Kinshasa. Fighting in its streets has occurred as recently as 2007. For those who live there, the memory is still fresh and raw.

Today the capital teems with an estimated 11 to 12 million people (out of Congo's total 66 million). Masses of street children have swarmed the capital, orphans from war, or cast-outs from their families. They are transported *en masse* out of the capital periodically, no one knows to where. The capital has no street lights that I saw and few paved streets. The vast majority of the population is not formally employed. Each day millions struggle for a meal.

Such poverty is astonishing considering Congo is reportedly the richest country in the world for natural resources, with an estimated U.S. $24 *trillion* in diamonds and other mineral wealth.[5] The cell phone and laptop you use today may work because of minerals from the Congo. Much of this wealth is being plundered by outsiders. The mineral-rich eastern Congo in particular is a natural magnet for refugees and rebels from numerous smaller neighboring countries.

When Rwanda's 1994 genocide was halted, thousands of killers fled into eastern Congo, finding remote Congolese villages easy to terrorize and plunder. When fighting erupted in Uganda, rebel soldiers from there also found refuge in eastern Congo. These included the evil warlord Joseph Kony and members of his "Lord's Resistance Army," who took child soldiers and perpetrated despicable acts. Another set of rebel soldiers from Burundi also settled there.

Some of these rebel soldiers are still looting the area's gold and diamond mines to fund their exploits. And, as rebels accustomed to blood and rampage, they do not hesitate to also murder, rape, and mutilate local citizens. Renegade militias and soldiers from the Congo itself, who are not paid regularly by the dysfunctional government, have also tried to cash in. Though the murders and rapes have lessened since Africa's "World War," they have not ceased. A ravaged, displaced population struggles to rebuild their lives and many still live in fear.

The brutality in Eastern Congo has given it the evil moniker: "the rape capital of the world." Rapes are inflicted with sticks and guns, too, tearing women's bodies so that blood, feces, and urine drain down their legs, with a stench that makes them outcasts.

A few days before I was due to leave for the Congo, I went on the U.S. State Department website for that country. It said crime was rampant even in the capital. The army itself sets up roadblocks for bribes. Westerners were advised not to go anywhere alone. Nighttime ventures were discouraged. All very sobering.

I flew into the DRC at night with another person visiting the microloan agency, Hope International.[6] The Kinshasa airport was dirtier and more chaotic than any I'd seen in Africa. I was on full alert. To my relief, we were met by the African director of Hope International there, a natural leader big enough to be a body guard, and arrived without incident at our hotel.

WITCHCRAFT AND DEATH

The next day I received an introduction to the country from an American named Jill (last name withheld), a dynamic leader who works with women at risk for prostitution, including widows. She told me she and her husband have lived in the Congo for years and have been evacuated twice due to fighting, including in their front yard. With both evacuations, they lost everything they owned in the Congo. But they'd come back twice and stayed, raising their children there, even after Jill and her son were carjacked by armed thugs.

Jill gave me some background on what widows experience there. "In the Congo, all causes of death are seen as spiritual," she said. "None are believed to be natural deaths or from illness. People go to a witchdoctor and have a ceremony done to 'eat a man's soul.' As soon as kids or adults get sick, people think witchcraft caused it.

"There's always fighting when a death happens. People say, 'Who's the witch among us?' This is especially true if there is a stepchild or cousin living with the family. Many of the street kids in Kinshasa have been kicked out for reasons like this."

> *Her husband's family blamed her for his death. They beat her, kicked her out.*

Even people who are respected may be blamed for deaths, she said. "I know of a widow whose husband was a pastor and chief. He was well respected. After he died, her husband's family blamed her for his death. They beat her, kicked her out, and took all she had." Jill also told me about a particular widow she knew who'd had no one to help her. The only "help" this widow received was from those who sent male visitors to her hut. The widow was then given food for her "services" to these men.

Another widow Jill knew had been married to a university professor. They lived in university housing and even had a personal car, which is rare in the Congo. When the husband died, his wife was expecting her third or fourth child. Even so, his family found a way to throw her out of her housing and took all she had. She survived by working as a maid.

In a way, Jill said, Congolese women are liberated, at least in the villages. "Women are soldiers, pastors, policemen. Even one in 20 chiefs in Congo is a woman." But sexual preying, she said, is still common.

Polygamous marriages also complicate widows' lives. "Often in Congo," she said, "there is a second, third, or fourth wife. This is not allowed in the churches, but about half of the men who work in institutions have a secret second wife. So the man starts stealing from his first family to support the second wife and family. The siblings from the different wives hate each other. The wives hate each other. It gets complicated. I've heard men say, 'I wish I would have stuck with one wife.'" Jill said almost all the women in the Congo are struggling to survive economically. And widows tend to suffer the worst. "But if a widow can build a small business," Jill concluded, "she has some hope for herself and her children."

MICROLOAN WIDOWS

One day in the Congo I met a group of widows at a microloan meeting. Most gatherings in this country, like this one, take place in churches, because those are the main buildings that can hold groups. When we first arrived, we were ushered in to sit in handmade wooden chairs at the front of the dirt-floor church. The front row just off to the side of us was filled with about six older women in colorful African dresses, sitting in a place of honor. I didn't know who they were. Some bustle was going on before the meeting would start, so I went over and shook each one's hand, as we smiled warmly at each other. They didn't speak English and I only knew one word in Lingala, their African language, which was *mbote,* hello. I used it repeatedly to greet each one.

The gracious woman who was the loan officer for this area for Hope International then made opening remarks. My twenty-something Congolese translator for the week, Emilie, filled me in. Then the widows were asked to come with me. To my delight, the front row of women I'd just greeted all stood up. We moved to wooden benches in the back of the church, and while the microloan meeting continued in the front of the church, the widows began telling me their stories. As they did, our little group of widows, many of whom had microloans, grew larger. More widows kept arriving to tell their stories too.

The first to speak, which was their culture of respect for elders, was one of the older widows. Their stories, with Emilie translating, gave a fascinating cross-section of life in the Congo and what it took for these widows to survive.

Henriette, 58: "Nobody in my husband's family helped me when my husband died of prostate problems. So I came here to seek for cash to do my business to care for my family. I sell second-hand cloth."

Jane, 53: "My husband died six years ago and left me with eight children. His family didn't help me but didn't take anything from me either. But there wasn't peace with my husband's family so I moved. I sell bread and fish. It is very, very difficult. My business is up and down."

Constantine, 48: "I was left with six children when my husband died. His family took all my belongings and I went to live with my own family members. Then I joined this group to get some cash to do some business. Now I am renting a house with that and selling bread and fish."

Widows in the DR Congo

Odette, 50: "I became a widow at age 36 with three children. I also cared for my late sister's two children. My husband's family took all my husband's belongings and left me with mine. They did not help me at all and insulted me. My parents decided to bring me back to their compound. My father is very, very old, so he does nothing. I am helping them. My business now is selling bread, maize, and giving loans to people of clothes and other items." Then, apparently thinking I had something to do with the running of the microloans, she asked for longer repayment terms! I had to smile. She was gutsy.

Antoinette, 56: I thought she was really beautiful and told her that through Emilie. She replied she was beautiful by God's grace. Good answer, I thought. She also told me more about her life than the others. "My husband died 20 years ago when I was 36. My husband was suffering in his feet. Before he died, we sold everything [probably to survive as a family.] He left me with seven children, from 11 years down to three months. The first ten years were tragic. I suffered a lot after the death of my husband."

"Did your husband's family help?" I asked, which of course is expected culturally. "Heh!" she said, implying not at all, turning her head away with disgust.

Widows in the DR Congo

"Apart from that," she continued, "I was working as a civil servant, but I was not well paid. At that time I was paid 30,000 Congolese francs [about U.S. $25] a month. We were renting a house. My children left school because I couldn't pay. The oldest didn't even complete his studies. Now he's living in Congo-Brazzaville.

"The second is a soldier. He started that at age 14. He decided to be engaged as a soldier because he had nothing to do but volunteer for Kabila's army. [Kabila is the country's president, preceded by his father.] Now he's living with the family. Thanks to our prayers he came back home.

"My salary wasn't sufficient to take care of my family and pay for a house so my church helped me a lot. I'm a Catholic believer.

"Now, thanks to a loan from Hope, I am selling bread and other items. I am also still working as a civil servant. I work as a cashier in a big hospital in Kinshasa, so I work two jobs."

Her children rarely go to school, because it is difficult to pay school fees. Even at a government school, the family must pay for uniforms and other costs that are prohibitively expensive for most people.

Widows in the DR Congo

Clementine, 60: "I became a widow in 1975. Since my husband died, his family abandoned me and took everything. They sent me out with my children. I had six children and the youngest was six. Now I am buying fruit and cooking tea to sell in the morning on the street."

Bivienne, 47: "My husband died two years ago. My late husband's family doesn't care about me and my child."

Anne Mary, 48: "I had eight children when I was widowed, 18

133

years old down to two months. We were living in Kisangani during Kabila's war." I asked if she saw fighting there and she said she had. "When we left to come to Kinshasa, my husband died. Then my late husband's family took everything. They left me only with the children. I was selling even my own clothes to care for my children." I noticed she was the most poorly dressed of all the women.

"My oldest child died last year. She was poisoned. We don't know how." Emilie explained that in eastern Congo it is common for people to be poisoned.

At that point, I asked one of the women from eastern Congo if she knew anyone who'd been raped there, and she said, "Of course!" The other women sitting around nodded their heads, and I could see I had a moment of losing credibility with them for even asking the question. It's probable some of them had been raped too.

Veronique, 51: (She surprised us when she began speaking in English – Emilie would get a rest from translating.) "I was widowed eight years before. When my husband died, we are living in a family compound. They decided to sell the compound and sent me out. I was a civil servant," but with a shift of political authorities, she said, "they sent people out." Then she surprised me when she said she now has an NGO (non-governmental organization). "After the death of my husband, I and my friends founded it. Most of the ones we try to help are jobless and widows. They are in the countryside, the poorest area.

"We encourage them, show them activities. We teach them also that after the death of the husband, you have to get up and work for your children. You have to believe in God. Now I am studying theology [she would be one of the few women able to do so in this part of the world].

They left me only with the children. I was selling my own clothes to care for them.

134

I need the diploma. I want to show God is good, that he cares for people.

"I have goats. We sell them. It is difficult to pay school fees. I have a loan from Hope. We are buying animals, selling grains to feed animals. I now have my fourth loan with Hope."

Then I asked her gently if she knew of many women who have been raped. "Of course. We do have some. We are fighting violence against women."

Veronique came across as intelligent and savvy and conducted herself with a graceful combination of humility and strength. The name of her NGO was in French, but she translated it into Forum of Women.

Then I turned to the group of widows still sitting around on the rows of wooden benches in the back of the church. I asked them if they met in groups in the churches. One widow I'd just interviewed spoke up and said she was the president of the widows in her church. "We pray together and we share our concerns. If there is a problem, we collect for the widow and visit one another." But obviously many were so poor that the collections must have been meager.

Another said her church had no such group. Then she added, "We have two categories of widows here. Well living and have nothing. Even no tea in the morning. They have nothing."

After prompting, one of the oldest women began to pray fervently out loud. "As you did with the Israelites," she pleaded with her God, "do for us!" She was likening the plight of widows in the Congo to the Israelites who were suffering under oppression in Egypt under Pharaoh and, like them, crying out for deliverance.

We drove away with much to think about. Riding along at a quick clip, I saw a woman lying face down in the dirt in someone's front yard. A crowd was gathered around her. But no one was turning her over or touching her. Why? Was she dead? Passed out? Beaten? Sick with no money for medicine and now gone? Just another casualty in the Congo? A widow? I still see her faded navy and tan-striped top, her western-style pants, her face embedded in the dirt so that she could not breathe. Maybe mid-30s. For a long time afterward, I wondered about her.

MARKET WIDOW

After a simple lunch of river fish at a restaurant, we went to Congo's largest market. I remembered fondly the last market I'd been to in Gulu, Uganda, how the rich colors of fresh tomatoes and vegetables in a peaceful setting delighted me. It was not to be so in Kinshasa's largest market, called Liberte. That means "freedom" in the French spoken by many here since Belgian colonial days. But the market is so crowded it has the nickname "Little China." We were going in to meet some microloan clients.

We pulled up to a chaotic entrance. People all around seemed desperate to earn enough money to feed their families that night. "You must leave all your bags in the car," Katie said to us from the front passenger seat. "It's too dangerous to take anything in. It would make us targets for thieves."

Are we sure we really want to go in to this place, then? I thought to myself.

But I trusted Katie. After a moment to adjust our bags, the van door opened, the sound level throbbed upward, and we entered the teeming masses. Our Congolese staff escort, a smart wiry young man, led us at a quick, no-nonsense pace. Another staff person followed behind us. We had orders not to be more than a few steps away from our escorts at all times. It's a potentially dangerous market for anyone at any time, but at the end of the day when it's that busy, we were told, it's particularly dangerous for foreigners, who are all seen as wealthy.

We stepped as rapidly as we could over trash and lots of refuse on the ground. Unpleasant smells assailed us. I'd never seen such a dirty market in Africa.

We stopped first at the little table of a woman selling fish. She beamed with pride over her business, started with the help of a microloan. Our presence quickly attracted a curious crowd. Among them was an older woman whose face seemed permanently etched with a look of horror and pain. I can only imagine what she must have suffered.

At a booth nearby sat another microloan client, a seamstress. Beatrice, a nice looking young woman of about 35, sat at an old sewing machine with the name "Singer" almost totally worn off, sewing a bright yellow printed fabric into ruffles for a child's dress. She stopped the foot peddle of the machine and looked up at us. I had the impression she was pressured to get the piece of clothing done. But she told us courteously about her sewing business. I asked our translator to find out if she was a widow. She was and she told us her story.

"In 2006 my husband died. He had a bad cold and died of a sinus infection." Can you actually die of a sinus infection, I wondered? But with such poverty and poor air quality in the market, perhaps respiratory illnesses can become dire, especially without money for medicine. "We grew up in a village. When my husband died, his family did not help us. I had to leave the village. They didn't let me take anything."

"When my husband died, I can't even send my children to school. I have four children, ages 18, 17, 13, and 6. I tried to start a

When my husband died, I had to leave the village. They didn't let me take anything.

business, but had nothing till Hope. Now I have had four loans. The first child has completed high school studies. Three are still in high school. I have three girls and a boy.

"I want them to have our own house. Now I am sharing one room with my children. I pray God for money to buy a house for me and my children."

We needed to let her get back to work. But the thought came to me to ask her to pray for the book I was writing that it might help many widows. Immediately after translation, she grabbed a piece of the bright yellow ruffled fabric lying nearby and covered her head with it. That was her prayer tradition, I realized, to pray with covered head, and she solved that quickly with her sewing at hand.

With her head down and covered by the fabric, I could not see her face. But I could hear her praying intensely in her language. I was surprised by how long she prayed. Toward the end of her prayer she gestured with her hands, shaking them up and down for emphasis. Then she was done. She uncovered her face and looked up at us. Her face was wet with tears. It was a poignant and beautiful sight all at once. She knew the suffering of widows. I was struck by the solidarity she exhibited with other widows in that moment, praying not just for herself, but for the help of all widows in Africa. It was important enough to her to let her sewing sit for a while.

Before we left, I asked the seamstress through Emilie, "May I put your story in my book that hopefully will help many widows?" After translation, Beatrice looked up and with a big smile, the first real joy I'd seen her have, she said, "Why not?" This was a common African phrase indicating a yes with pleasure.

In the van driving away, Emilie and I talked about what we'd just experienced. Emilie's tone became a bit fevered, and suddenly she exclaimed, "It happened to my mother too! They chased us away!

I was 12 when my father died. We had a good house and money! But his family took *everything!*" Her voice grew louder with grief and outrage. "We lived in Equateur, a province. My father had a big house and we had many things!

It happened to my mother too! They chased us away! I was 12 when my father died.

"Then when my father died, his brother came to chase us away. He told us one time to go and we resisted. The third time he came, my mother said I don't want them to kill you because of a house. So we left.

"My mother suffered a lot. She was man-less. For a while we lived with my mother's father. Then my grandfather also died. When I was 14, my cousin in Kinshasa took me in and I left my mother's house. When I was 20, my mother died. I have one sibling living with me and two are living with my aunt. By God's grace I am alive and completed my studies."

I sat there stunned. Even Emilie. I was surprised and I wasn't. It happened all over Africa, to the poor and not so poor.

PROFESSIONAL WOMEN WEIGH IN

One evening while in the DRC I hosted four professional women, an uncommon commodity in that country, at my hotel's simple restaurant. The organizer of the evening's group, Marie Dilu-Munsi, has an association that trains women who have small businesses. I was honored when she told me she had worn the same stunning African dress with sparkling adornments to meet me that she'd worn to speak to the U.S. Congress in Washington, D.C.

Her association includes widows, abandoned women who live without a husband, and single women, who are all stigmatized in Congolese (and African) society. "They walk alone," Marie said.

"They have no security. They face life alone with no support. Banks look at you as vulnerable, with no attachments. It's hard to get loans. Nobody trusts you."

Angele Mbuyi Bipenduke, also at our dinner, is part of an association of women lawyers that has written pamphlets to bring awareness to women about their legal rights. "Most of the time," she said, "women here don't know their rights. Or if they do know, the husband's family doesn't care. And marriage for succession [where the widow can actually inherit upon her husband's death] must be officially, legally done for the women to have any rights."

Josephine Ngalula, another dynamic woman at our table, works on gender violence. "Most of the time, women don't know they have to get married legally with a document instead of only in a traditional ceremony. A woman may be in a marriage 20 or 30 years and not know her marriage isn't legal. Even if she's married legally," she agreed with Angele, "she probably doesn't know the law. And when a woman does start to claim her rights, they may accuse her of witchcraft, that she killed her husband. They chase her away."

"When the husband dies," Angele, the attorney, explained, "the wife only has rights to what has been agreed upon before the marriage. Even women who know their rights are afraid to face the man's family. And if they do go before a tribunal, the judge may not even show in the court because of corruption. We have some women who are judges, but the government appoints the judges. And women are few in government – only 8%. Under [President] Mobutu, we got women in politics and our first female ambassador. But there is no effort to promote women. We have a long way to go."

They walk alone. They have no security. They face life alone with no support.

With women like these in the Congo, though, there is hope.

140

I was glad I'd gone to the heart of Africa, the Congo. Here "hearts of darkness" (as the author Joseph Conrad termed them in his classic book more than 100 years before) had raped

When a woman does start to claim her rights, they may accuse her of witchcraft.

the Congo of its earthly riches. People with dark hearts were still doing so to acquire minerals for our cell phones and laptops. But I'd found Congo's other riches: her courageous widows.

RETURNING HOME

On the trip home, I started getting sick. It was the only time of all my trips to Africa this happened. But I'd forgotten one of my cardinal rules and eaten a salad on the plane that looked delicious but was made in Africa under conditions I didn't know about. Also, I'd foolishly eaten a sauce toward the end of the 17-hour flight that looked curdled. In the night at my cousin's home outside Washington, D.C., the malady hit me in earnest. That long night, I kept thinking about the millions of Congolese who died of disease not that long ago in "Africa's World War," fleeing their homes, hiding in the malaria-infested bush, not having good food or water. I thought especially about the many widows and their children who often have no one to help them when sick.

Back home recovering, I did something unusual. I turned on daytime TV. And even more unusual for me, I turned on a channel with U.S. government committee hearings. I was astonished to see they were about the Congo! And there, testifying, was John Prendergast, who had spoken at my school when I was a Master's student. He has worked on human rights for Africa for over 25 years. Joining him in testifying were a famous U.S. actor, Ben Affleck, and Cindy McCain, wife of a former U.S. presidential candidate. They were advocating for a special envoy to the Great Lakes area of Africa, of which the Congo is a part, to help address the huge needs there.

Just two days after I left the DRC, attackers broke into the presidential palace. Guards thwarted the assassination attempt and killed the attackers. Significant unrest followed in the streets of the capital. Katie told me the U.S. Embassy was advising U.S. citizens not to travel there for a while. I'd gotten in and out of the country just in time, in a rare opportunity to go with someone highly recommended, to hear the stories of the widows in the DR Congo. The man in the elevator had been right. It was very important their stories be told.

MBOTE!

Oh, God, am I really lying face down here in the dirt? I cannot move. Life is pouring out of my body. Can this be? And here in the yard of this man? He hates me! All I did was help his wife when he beat her. She came to me so many nights. I held her while she cried and moaned. She was safe with me. Then one night she came no more.

So many men beat their women. No one even cared when my friend died from the beatings of that bad man's hands.

I wanted that man to suffer. I wanted him to change. I pounded on your heaven for days and days. For you to take that man in your hands. To do something. But you did not do anything to him. And then that man beat his next wife too. After a long time, I gave up crying out to you. God, why did you turn your ears and eyes away from us? From me and from her? I would like to ask you that when I go to your home.

I cannot move. Maybe a doctor at the big hospital could have fixed me. My side hurt so badly. But I had no money for that. They make you show your money at the gate to the hospital or they won't let you in. The mean guard smells of khat leaves and palm wine. He would have shooed me away. Every day he wears those whitish pants and shirt, like they could make his dark spirit clean. Eh, he did his job. Just that I could forgive. But he was cruel to so many. Like another friend who was a widow.

One night I took her to that gate. She was leaning on me like a heavy weight. She was full of pain and fever. I moved her with all the strength I could find in my arms. She had the shaking and heat from the malaria. All the way there I prayed the guard would let us in. I prayed for a miracle. God, didn't you hear me? I prayed that guard would greet my friend with proper respect. She was such a good person. That he would say respectfully, "Mbote, Mama, come on in!" But that guard knew we had no money. He snarled at us like a mean dog to go away. His spit from chewing the khat leaves flew our way when he yelled at us. Like a snake's venom. His words shot into my heart like the fangs of an adder snake that kills you. Anger and tears came out of me. I could not save her.

She died the next night. She was lying on her old mattress on the floor. It was the only thing in her one room with the dirt floor. Her children wailed around her. They threw back their heads, and the pain in their hearts beat them up. They cried so long that they held their sides and then fell on the dirt floor to cry some more.

I stayed with them that first night. But I had no more room in my one room to take them home with me. My children were still there. My old aunty too. They took up all the floor space with me at night. I could not put another person in that small room. I could not take more children. I went to them each day for a while to bring them a little food. My children needed it and grew more and more hungry.

I knew the children of my friend were afraid by themselves. I cried every night for a month that I could not help them or find anyone to help them. Too many orphans, too many. Can you ever forgive me, God? Those children could not pay money for that room any more. So they lived on the streets. The government soldiers came and took them away. Like many other children. I do not know where. I never saw them again.

Except, one day, a few years later, I thought I saw the oldest son. He was with the soldiers. He was using bad words. I could tell he lived a dark life. Our eyes found each other. Then his darted away. He turned and jumped on a crowded van bus. I think he was sad in his heart at his life now. Ashamed. Maybe I reminded him of his good Mama. But I would have forgiven him. I could help him some then too. My daughters and son had become full grown. And my aunty was now gone to your heaven to find her youth once again. But I never saw the son of my friend after that.

I do not want to hate that guard, God. The one who turned us away from the hospital. But blackness is living in my heart toward him. Please help me. I don't want to hate him, and wear the black clothes of hatred, especially now, when I may be seeing you soon.

Will your guard let me in to your heaven? I have tried to help others, but so many I could not help. Will I see my neighbor who died at your home? And dear friend? And the baby I surrendered to you, lifeless, when he was just three months living? And my mother? Oh, God, it is still painful to think of how she died. The terrible night the soldiers came to our village where I grew up in eastern Congo. How I miss her so . . . .

Mama, did my life put happiness in your heart? I was not as good as you were to everyone. Will you wait for me at the hut that is ours in heaven? Are you cooking my favorite groundnut soup over a fire? Does that fire burn without the sticks I gathered every day for you, sometimes far from home?

Will I see you soon now, mama? Here I am in just this old striped top and jeans. But it's strange. I feel like I am wearing the beautiful African dress you made for me with your own hands. How could that be? Oh, I loved the purple and green fabric. And the headdress! Remember how we laughed and danced around the first time I put it on? Oh, mama, now I know you will wrap me in your arms warm and tight once again. You will love me no matter what. I feel a big smile inside me when I think of that. It is big and lush inside me like the tall bean plants that grew outside our home.

"It's Fazila! Is she gone?" someone in the crowd gathered around said. "Eh!" another wailed. "She was such a good person! She always cared for others. This is a terrible way for her to go. Why would this happen to such a good person?"

Just then, the man who owned the property returned from selling the cook stove of a neighbor who owed him money and could not pay. The man had stormed in and grabbed that cook stove, not caring how the family would eat.

Now he saw the crowd of a dozen or so people circled around something on the dirt outside his home. He was annoyed they were on his property. Then, as he pressed rudely in between them to see what was in the circle, he saw the woman lying face down on the dirt. Suddenly he recognized her. She was the one who had helped his second wife when he beat her!

"Fazila is dead!" a woman spat out the words to him. She knew how it would affect him. "She died here on the dirt by your house!" In an instant he felt the horror! This was a curse he could never escape! She had died on his land! Was it because he had beaten his wife to death? He beat away the thought like he had hands inside his head. Then he started running recklessly down the busy road in front of his house. But he'd had a bit too much to drink already from the profits of the cook stove and could not run fast. He stumbled and fell trying. His head and face hit rocks as he lunged face down and he began to bleed. The gash in his head gave forth torrents of blood like the big river running at the edge of the city.

He felt a sudden alarm that this beating to his head from the big rock could take away his life. "Oh, God, give me another chance! I will give that woman a proper burial! I will change!" Then he felt a sudden strength come into his arms, and he lifted himself up to go care for the body of Fazila.

WESTERN SAHARA
MOROCCO
TUNISIA
ALGERIA
LIBYA
EGYPT
MAURITANIA
MALI
NIGER
CHAD
SUDAN
ERITREA
DJIBOUTI
GAMBIA
SENEGAL
GUINEA
BISSAU
GUINEA
BURKINA FASO
BENIN
TOGO
NIGERIA
SOUTH
SUDAN
ETHIOPIA
SIERRA
LEONE
LIBERIA
COTE
D'IVOIRE
GHANA
CENTRAL AFRICAN
REPUBLIC
EQUATORIAL
GUINEA
CAMEROON
SOMALIA
GABON
CONGO REPUBLIC
DEMOCRATIC
REPUBLIC OF
THE CONGO
UGANDA
RWANDA
BURUNDI
KENYA
CABINDA
TANZANIA
COMOROS
ANGOLA
MALAWI
MADAGASCAR
ZIMBABWE
MOZAMBIQUE
NAMIBIA
BOTSWANA
SWAZILAND
LESOTHO
SOUTH
AFRICA

NORTH AFRICA
SUB-SAHARAN
AFRICA

ZAMBIA

7

BREAKTHROUGH
IN ZAMBIA

*"Cursed is anyone who withholds
justice from... the widow."*

The Bible[1]

Ever since I'd heard that pastors in Zambia were preaching at funerals about not harming widows – and this was causing a decrease in property grabbing, I wanted to go there. Funerals are major events throughout Sub-Saharan Africa, and this could be a breakthrough not only for Zambia but for Africa.

The majority of Sub-Saharan Africa professes Christianity. In Zambia, for example, it's estimated at 85%.[2] The country even has a constitutional amendment saying it is a Christian nation (while still providing for freedom of religion).[3] And the Bible has many passages about helping and not harming widows. If more pastors preached these at funerals, challenging the cultural norm, the lives of many widows, and their children, could be transformed.

Formerly Northern Rhodesia, Zambia gained its independence from Britain in 1964 and took its new name from the Zambezi River, meaning "God's river." The country now has a reputation for political stability and a relatively efficient government. It's considered generally peaceful and trouble-free. This is quite a contrast to hotbed neighbors like the DR Congo and Angola. Zambia's biggest troubles in the last few decades have come from a worldwide drop in the price of copper, its principal export. Some of my friends in humanitarian organizations have told me that if they could live any place in Africa, they would choose Zambia, because of its stability, friendly people, and natural beauty.

A wide variety of wildlife in large game parks draws tourists, as does magnificent Victoria Falls, the largest waterfall in the world. It was named by David Livingstone, the famous Scottish explorer and medical missionary who worked to end the slave trade in his beloved Africa. Legend has it his heart was buried in Zambia under an *mvula* tree, and the rest of his body with kings in London's Westminster Abbey.

Zambia, though, has one of the highest death rates in the world from widow maker and taker HIV/AIDS. The rate is currently 13.5% of adults, actually a decrease from the prior decade but still too high.[4] And many Zambians, like people across Africa, are poor. Malnutrition is such a serious problem it is said to stunt growth in more than half of Zambia's children.[5] Malaria is also endemic and a major cause of death.[6]

In the midst of this grim reality, widows are some of the worst off. Although Zambia has better inheritance laws than many countries in Sub-Saharan Africa, and a human rights commission to hear grievances, which most countries in the region currently do not, tribal practices still cause problems. Reportedly, 78% of widows and orphans countrywide suffer injustice.[7]

A friend who did some work in Zambia but didn't know of my interest in the country invited me one day "out of the blue" to meet her there. A few days before I was to leave, though, I injured my shoulder and had my arm in a sling. I wondered how I would manage traveling. The first place I needed to lift my luggage was at the security line at my local airport. The woman ahead of me turned and said, "I know you! We just met at the documentary about Liberian women."[8] Noticing the sling on my arm, she turned to her strapping son of 17 and said, "Help her with her bags!" I hadn't even needed to ask. Once again, my quest to tell the widows' stories was facilitated.

BISHOP BANDA

One of the pastors speaking out on behalf of widows in Zambia is Bishop Joseph Banda, senior pastor of a large church in the capital. When I met him, he seemed intelligent, professional, and genuine.

"Over the last 15 years" he began, "we've conducted various programs to be socially engaged in the society. In 1999, my wife, Gladys, began an outreach to street children. Then we acquired 14 acres of farmland to build a community school with 400 children and started a mother's program with land for the women. After that, we reached out to commercial sex workers and began an outreach to those who were HIV positive. We now have 4,000 people currently on some kind of care.

"Around 2003 or 2004, we began work with land rights. IJM [International Justice Mission] helped us form a trust for a vulnerable family in our church where both parents had passed away and people wanted to grab the property. Since then we have done workshops with IJM so people can learn about their land rights, intestate succession laws, and inheritance rights. We also sometimes meet with families about land issues. We include persons from the man's side of the family and the wife's side. Then together they can decide what to do. If there's a will, sometimes the family respects that. Sometimes they won't. Representatives from our church will also go and sit with families to help them select an administrator of the estate.

"We've had several people speaking openly about the dangers and evils of property grabbing. We challenge families to avoid the aggravation. We talk about these issues at funerals. We encourage them to be civil about discussions of what will happen with property when a family member dies. We encourage the man's family to leave a legacy, an imprint in those children. Even if others have a right to a part of that land [Zambian law allows for the husband's parents to receive a share], we encourage them to give it up for the sake of the children.

"We have had challenges and problems," the Bishop said. "Sometimes people don't want to look at what is good for others. Sometimes you have to be patient. But we encourage them to consider other family members for the good of their name and their integrity. Even some women outside the church have come to us for help."

When I asked Bishop Banda if he quotes the parts of the Bible at funerals that talk about treating widows well, he said "absolutely." Over a dozen strong passages about widows are available for him to draw on. I was astonished as I assembled these passages at how much importance is placed on the good treatment of widows, and how angry God gets when widows are ill-treated. Statements like:

"Cursed is anyone who withholds justice from...the widow."[9]

"Woe to those who...withhold justice from the oppressed of my people, making widows their prey."[10]

One passage even equates true religion with helping widows!

We encourage the man's family to leave a legacy for the sake of the children.

"Religion that God our Father accepts as pure and faultless is this: to look after orphans and widows in their distress...."[11]

Then I asked him what is needed to address this land rights problem at a societal level for widows and their children. He replied without hesitation. "First, a general awareness of the fact

Most important, he said, is to find ways to empower these widows economically.

that these women have some God-given rights prescribed in national laws too. Secondly, an awareness of the availability of institutions like the church and IJM.

"Most important is to find ways to empower these widows economically. We've given them access to the church's land to grow cash crops. We give them training in how to run a small business. We advocate now for grants given in groups. We help these individuals see they can help themselves. Then their self-worth is improved. They have to be empowered."

LAND RIGHTS TRAINING

The next morning I went to a training by IJM about land rights for women at a smaller church in a poor but bustling neighborhood. It was a beautiful sunny day. The front step to the church was a large rock, and it tilted a bit as I stepped on it to enter through the single narrow opening. But I felt such a joy at being there to see this breakthrough training I could have skipped over the unsteady rock. The church had nice wide proportions, open sides with no windows, curtains of a gold-colored, polyester-like material billowing at the front, plastic chairs, wooden benches, and a dirt floor. All in all, a very pleasant place.

The whole neighborhood was invited. Mostly women attended. They appeared to be in their 20s and 30s, and poor but still attractive in their colorful African dresses.

The workshop began with a few joyful songs led by someone from the packed church. Most of the singing was in the local language,

153

but I didn't need the translation to grasp the joy, or relief at being in a safe, uplifting place for a time that could positively impact lives.

Maimbo Ziela, a dynamic attorney with IJM, had no problem engaging the audience. She began with a little quiz to test our knowledge of what Zambian laws said about land inheritance. What is the surviving spouse entitled to? What if there are multiple wives? How many people need to witness a will? Other IJM staff spoke too, including some men. Most of the speaking was in the local language, but they did some going back and forth in English, too.

They also gave the attendees a handout called "Guide to the Law of Succession," a treasure in legal guidance for poor young women in particular who might face battles of their own. If there is no will, Zambia's law divides assets among the widow and her children and, reflecting the culture, the husband's family. The children get half, the widow gets 20%, and any other dependents 10%. In the case of multiple wives, each one's share is based on the length of her marriage and her contribution toward acquisition of the property. Then the parents of the deceased husband get 20% of the assets. Before the law was enacted, they had the right to take all, down to pots, pans, and clothing.

An administrator for the estate named by the family or specified in the will makes the judgment calls within the above, such as how much each child or multiple wife gets. No wonder Bishop Banda and his church staff would help with the selection of an administrator when they had the opportunity to do so.

IJM staff also gave out a sample one-page will and covered when a will is valid, who may make a will, who may witness it, the duties of an administrator to carry out the will, how disputes are handled, and penalties for an administrator fraudulently disposing of trust property—seven years in jail! More African countries could do with such motivating penalties. Excitement in the room grew as attendees asked questions and began to understand their legal rights. The information was "brass tacks," empowering, and much needed.

Somewhere along the line I also picked up a full-color pamphlet called "Property Grabbing! What You Need to Know." The front cover showed an angry man talking and pointing to a woman while he was holding a document. The pamphlet had simple, one-line answers about inheritance laws, what happens to a widow when there is no will, and imprisonment penalties for property grabbers. This is just what unscrupulous and threatening people may not have known and need to be told. The back page had a picture of a dejected, poor child with the caption: "Property grabbers bring misery to widows and children!" More African countries need this kind of publicity.

WIDOWS AT THE TRAINING

After the training, I spontaneously interviewed two of the women who'd just attended it, both widows. We stood outside the church on the dirt under a lovely old tree with dark green leaves as the breeze blew and babies cried in the background. Stacks of tan building blocks sat between many small houses, and an outhouse with a blue piece of cloth over the entrance flapped in the breeze. Bushes with white flowers bloomed around the poor neighborhood. I could see happy children running up to the vehicle I'd come in, peering in, perhaps hoping for a candy.

One of the IJM staff, a gentle giant type of man, began to translate for my interviews. He wore a t-shirt saying, "The world is my neighbor." He was perfect for IJM.

To my delight, the first widow was a striking woman of about age 50 I'd seen sitting in the back of the church, highlighted with sunlight and listening intently to the teaching. She had a stately bearing and was dressed in lovely African attire. Unfortunately, I did not get her name.

"She stayed with her husband in the city," my translator said. "When he died, she went to her own village where she grew up, not the husband's village. So that's a variation from the usual way they get married and go within one area and remain there for their lives. She had left her children [with the man's family]. They are all since grown. She is adjusting."

She seemed so sad then, and I wondered why she would leave her children. Had her husband's family chased her away and kept the children, as they had the right culturally to do? Asking her to explain, with her standing there unexpectedly outside the church with no prior connection to any of us, seemed insensitive. I thanked her as kindly as I could for speaking with me.

Another widow was waiting to talk to me, more gregarious and comfortable. Her name was Dorothy. She wore a simple scarf tied on her head and a charcoal-colored corduroy jacket over a African-patterned dress. I thought her to be in her 50s.

"Her husband died in 2000," the IJM translator said. I asked him if he would inquire whether she had lost land when her husband died.

"Aah," she sighed, smiling in resignation and turning her head away.

The translation continued. "They managed to get *all* the things she had. They had taken her property, but she didn't

Dorothy

follow up on it because she was scared.

As soon as she heard the translation, she smiled and threw her head back in laughter.

"They got the property, and after they sold that, they didn't share the money with her accordingly. But she managed to sell her house before they could come in and take it. She took her portion from the house and put it in another house, a two-room house where she was staying with her children. None of the relatives came back to take care of her or her children. She stays alone. She's not trading or doing anything. She just relies on people who assist her, including the son-in-law and daughters. She's also taking care of her mother, who's almost 99 years old and can't walk. She gets support from well-wishers and some of her children." When Dorothy talked about caring for her mother, she teared up.

Dorothy has HIV/AIDS. "Do you take ARVs?" I asked. She nodded yes.

"She is on ARVs. Even one of her children is on ARVs. He's 17 years old."

She seemed uncomfortable then, so to change the subject, I asked what she had been afraid of if she tried to get the property back. She was afraid, she said, of being bewitched and killed. She was not a Christian then but is now. I asked if she fears witchcraft now. As soon as she heard the translation, she smiled and threw her head back in laughter. For the first time I saw her beautiful full mouth of straight teeth, like so many Africans. She repeated a short phrase twice in her African language, pointing her finger upward for emphasis with a smile.

"No! She only fears God!" The translator explained, a phrase often used in Africa to mean a healthy respect for God, not a negative fear.

157

"Yes, me too!" I responded. We all laughed together and said our goodbyes.

UN SPEAKER AND A PIECE OF CLOTH

The next day I had the honor of meeting with the person who changed my life with her ten-minute speech at the United Nations (as told at the beginning of this book). Elizabeth Mataka had spoken with eloquence and gravitas on how widows in Sub-Saharan Africa often lose land and belongings when husbands die. Born in Botswana, married and settled in Zambia, she was then the Global Ambassador for HIV/AIDS for the United Nations. To my astonishment, my friend who invited me to Zambia was hosting a reception while I was there honoring Mrs. Mataka. When people at the reception began speaking up to honor her, I too gave thanks before the group for her influence on my life and this book.

My friend also took several of us from the reception to visit a group of HIV/AIDS-positive women, some of whom were widows. They were tie-dyeing cloth and gave us a demonstration on an outdoor concrete floor surrounded by wooden racks covered with pieces of material for sale, all beautifully dyed and stamped with attractive African designs and colors.

Another woman and I both became interested in the same piece of cloth. Immediately, she unselfishly backed off to let me have it. Then I noticed how the cloth matched her blue eyes perfectly. "Kathryn," I told her, "if I get this cloth, every time I wear it I'll think how it matches your eyes. No, this is your piece of cloth." My "sacrifice" was nothing like that of Aunty Margaret's friend who had given her half of a piece of cloth, but it still gave joy.

Before we left, I started an impromptu dance with the tie-dyers' children gathered around to see us off. I knew some of them were "orphans" who had watched their widowed mothers bury their fathers. For those brief moments, we were freed from life's

cares and found respite together
dancing in each other's joy.

A WIDOW PREVAILS

While in Zambia, I met with
a widow who had personally
benefited from IJM's teaching
to pastors about land rights.
Armed with legal knowledge
from a pastor, this widow had
fought and won to keep her land,
without having to go to court.

Matilda

Her name was Matilda, and we met at the IJM offices in Lusaka.
She wore a western-style skirt suit and appeared better educated
than the other widows I'd interviewed. She was accompanied by
her mother, Monica, and by a pastor who was a friend of the family,
Bishop Felix Simuchimba.

Out of respect, I asked if he would say a prayer to begin our time
together. He began, "Father, it is you who has given the heart for
the widows...."

Matilda's story began like so many other accounts I'd heard:

"After my husband died, the very day after the funeral, his family
followed me up to my bedroom to get my husband's clothes. These
are called 'the clothes of the dead.' Three or four days later, both
sides of the family had a meeting. They never wanted to listen to
me at first. They wanted us to sell the farm and van.

"They also wanted 30% for my husband's mother [instead of the
20% provided by law]. They said this was because there were no
dependents [who get 10%]. I have two stepdaughters and four
children. They wanted to divide the amounts for the children.

"They wanted to see my husband's pay-slip. He was a maintenance manager with an airline. They took my ATM card. I had no money for food for my children. So my mother brought money for food for her daughter and grandchildren," Matilda said, referring to herself and her children.

"We had saved money for the children's school fees. But they took the ATM [card] so I had no access to it. It took three months to withdraw money from the account. My brother-in-law was the core administrator, and I was an administrator. My husband, his name was Wisdom, did not make a will, but he said his wishes before he died. He said his wife would be in charge." Obviously, though, that was not happening.

"Before my husband died, we had problems with my mother-in-law. She told my husband maybe his wife made him sick. Maybe she poisoned you." Matilda looked hurt and disgusted about this. "There was no peace in our home."

Then Bishop Simuchimba explained, "Some Africans believe you poisoned your husband to get the property from him. This accusation is very common, especially with HIV/AIDS."

"This was so sad for me," Matilda said. "I was unhappy for quite some time. His mother asked, 'Did you do this to my son? Maybe you did some potions [used for passion] wrongly.' I was so annoyed. My husband told me he took our car and hid it at that time.

"Then both families came together and for six months before my husband's death, there was peace at home. My husband knew his family would try to do land grabbing. So he set up two accounts, one for the children's education, and one account for building a building. He told me to use the money in the account for the children's school fees.

"My husband died of a heart problem. He was 49 years old. He had enlargement of the heart and became weak. I am 36. We were married 16 years.

I refused to sell the land they wanted. We bought it together. I worked for two years.

"It was not right for my husband's family to decide alone what would happen with our lives after he died. I refused to sell the land they wanted. We can farm with the land. It was just bare land. We bought it together. I worked for two years. I went to Swaziland. I was a clerical officer. After his death, I sold the van to finish building a guest house so we could rent it out to get some income.

"I was then summoned to the Human Rights Commission by my stepdaughter. She was being influenced by my husband's family. She'll be 20 this year. She wanted to know how things were divided. She wanted a share.

"The Human Rights Commission asked about the salary for my late husband, money for the farm. The Human Rights Commission said, 'You have four children under 18. It must be the last solution to sell the farm and house in Lusaka.'" So the Commission stood with Matilda.

"I do gardening now at the farm. It is a one-hour drive from here. We grow maize, vegetables, oranges, lemons, guavas, mango, *popo* [which I believe is papaya], bananas, avocado, spinach, and okra. We have two and one-half hectares," about six acres.

Then I asked the mother if she would also speak about what happened. I saw a sparkle come to her eyes. She was too polite to have intruded uninvited into her daughter's story, but I could tell she was pleased to be asked. It turns out she had a major role in Matilda's victory.

"It was a very difficult time as a family," she said, with Bishop

Simuchimba translating. "We consulted our family to sit together with the family of Matilda's husband.

"He had said his wife couldn't do such a thing as to hurt him, that perhaps the office people had bewitched him. He was ten months in and out of the hospital. On and off, in and out."

Then Bishop Simuchimba added, "Usually in Africa if the husband is sick, his family sends some family to help nurse him, but they didn't help her."

Monica continued. "The funeral was at his house. They took away the ATM card. Then Matilda had no food, no money, she was completely stranded. I was doing some business in town and took food to my daughter and grandchildren.

"I live at the farm. When my son-in-law passed away, it was bare land." I was amazed after hearing about all the things growing there now.

"When Matilda's husband died," the mother continued, "her children were 15 – a boy, 12 – a girl, 9 – a girl, and 2 – a boy." When they took her ATM card, they couldn't get the money, but they didn't want Matilda to have access to it.

"I learned about land rights. Bishop Simuchimba told me. Other widows told me. I go to a Catholic church and heard about land rights there too."

A VOICE FOR THE VOICELESS

Then Bishop Simuchimba spoke. He had a warm, kind manner but also an unmistakable strength and passion for helping others.

"I hope to be a voice. I see the kind of betrayal that goes on. Often wives don't see it coming. Matilda and her husband were living together for 16 years. They accumulated money. There was trust, love, one or two things shaking, but they were a team.

People are laughing, enjoying, then they turn on the widow. It is a shock to her.

"The in-laws don't show it, but at the last minute, there's a meeting after the death, sometimes the same day. They go through the estate. They find fault. Say the wife is the cause of the death. People are laughing, enjoying, then they turn on the widow. It is a shock to the widow.

"Matilda saw it coming in the last days of her husband's life. She is from an educated kind of a family.

"What motivates the husband's family to do this? They already have cars, etc. So what is their intention? They are seeking for more strength.

"There is stress when the man is sick. Often there are more single women than men, so a wise woman doesn't want to lose her husband. Week after week Matilda was at her husband's side in hospital. Then she was accused. By people she didn't even know. An aunt from a village comes.

"If a woman even raises her voice, she's seen as stubborn. She cannot defend her rights. Women can't voice out."

I asked Bishop Simuchimba why he was involved in helping widows. "With my sister," he replied, "they took everything. As Christians we decided to let it go, but that wasn't the right thing to do.

"When you live in the compounds, you know what is happening in the neighborhood. Before I was a pastor, I saw what was happening in families. Often it is the very women who suffer loss who are in the forefront of grabbing. At this, he had a pained look on his face.

"The widow may be sickly. She may have nine or ten kids. There's always extended family too. The kids are attending to their mother. There is no school for them. The whole family is going down. Then the families grab that which can sustain the widows and children for food, for medical requirements.

"I did a course to counsel families, to be a voice. I work with victims, the police. I felt a call to be a voice to the voiceless. At my church we teach people, from the pulpit, in small meetings," like the one I'd attended the day before at a church. "We started up a Justice Department at our church.

"When there's a death, only families are at a meeting afterwards. And the men always have the upper hand. But I mention the Justice Department when I'm preaching, so now some families will permit a church member to attend the meeting.

"Matilda heard about me through her aunty. I knew her. They brought me to pray for the husband when he was ill. I prayed with the husband two to three times a week for four to six months. I was at the Copper Belt when he died. Then I discovered the problems Matilda was having.

"With my sister they took everything," he concluded with sorrow. "My sister had HIV when she died. The man knew and abandoned her. He brought another lady and there was a fight. I stayed with my sister for one year till she died."

No wonder Bishop Simuchimba had such a heart for widows. With clergy like him and Bishop Banda, and the one who had opened his church for the training I attended, widows could have breakthroughs instead of breakdowns. Africa needs many more like them.

HEADING HOME

The day I was to leave Zambia, my flight to Europe was delayed and then cancelled due to a massive ash cloud from a volcano in Iceland. Most of the people on my flight ended up stranded in Zambia for a week, but I was put on a packed flight. The only reason I can figure is my arm was still in a sling. Even that was used for good in my quest to tell the widows' stories!

ALL NIGHT LONG

All night long I have wept. How could today be the funeral of my man? He was young. Only 34. He could climb the trees to find food. He could lift me up in his arms like a child. Then he was sick. But I do not want to think of that. Or our six children, four boys and two girls... Who will care for them? And my oldest girl needs medicine for that cough!

My man worked hard. We had hopes and dreams. I believed our dreams could walk into our lives one day as real as the dawn rises on the Zambezi River with sweet pinkness. Now, it is all a bad dream.

What will happen after the funeral today? Will I be like the widow who lived next to us in the village where I grew up? Will I be chased away from my home after the funeral by my husband's family too? I can still hear her screams when they took sticks to her to make her go. I can still see the wide look in her eyes, like a lion was after her and she knew her legs could not outrun it but she must try. Only they did not want to catch her. Just to make her go.

I can still see the look of victory in their eyes when they saw her leave. They turned like strutting roosters to walk into her hut, still warm from her cook fire and smelling like her. I wanted to bat them away like I did the rooster when he bothered those poor hens too much. I could not believe what the people said, that the widow had eaten her husband's soul. Their souls were dark. True, the man did get sick and die. But his wife was always kind. She was kinder to me than my own mother who had more children to feed and clothe. Many nights I heard my mother cry herself to sleep from her hard life. My father would beat her after he drank palm wine with the men in the bad hut at the edge of the village.

Will anyone speak up for me? My husband's mother is not a bad person. But she is weak. She had to marry her husband's younger brother after her husband died. He did not love her and was very cruel to her. He broke her spirit like a twig snapped by an elephant in the forest. No, she will not speak up for me.

If my father still breathed life, would he come to my village and speak for me? No, for him a woman must make her way in her husband's village. The family of the husband must care for the children and widow. That is one way, but it doesn't always win. The greedy ones can win. They blame others for the darkness in their souls. No, not even my own father would speak for me. Is there anyone who will?

Should I rise up early and hide our clothes and cook pans in the forest? That way I can find them later if we must run. But oh, I am so weary, too weary now for that. I cannot lift my legs yet from my place on the ground in our hut. For days I nursed my husband till the end, hardly sleeping at all. This is the first I have been able to lay down for days. No, I cannot try to hide our things now.

Is there anyone who will speak up for me?

The village pastor was also sleepless that night . . .

All night I have cried out to my God. What will I say at today's funeral? The men will wear their black mourning wraps and the women will wail, like it was their own husband. And what will I do? Will I walk like in a dream, doing the same things, saying the same things we always do? Make the funeral as the pastor for this village like I usually do? And after the funeral that praises the man, what will happen to his widow?

I have seen what happens to many widows after the death of the husband. And I know this man's family. I have heard the men whispering behind the hut of the oldest brother. They plan to chase the widow away. They will take the land of her husband for themselves. Her yams are ready now. They will take them with big joy. The land of this man has always been the best. They wanted it for themselves. Now is their chance to grab it. They are hard in their hearts. I know they can do it.

I heard about a law in our country that the widow gets part of the land of her husband. But in our village it is not so.

The men take it all. They would laugh at the law. The women are afraid of a curse. They will not speak up for themselves. They are beaten if they do.

God, if I speak up for the widow, the men may beat me too. They will stop giving me the eggs and other things from each family for the village pastor and his family. How will my family live if I speak out? I ask you that! I know what your ancient book says about widows. I still have the old book my father had. He passed it to me when he lay dying. I took it as a great treasure. That is what it was to him. Now it is for me too. I find peace when I read it. And many of the villagers do too when they hear it. I read it to them after we have danced and swayed for joy under the big mvula tree that gives us shade. Then the limbs of that tree are like your arms over us, protecting us, comforting us. I love those times when we feel like you are there with us.

I know what the old book says about widows. Over and over again you say to protect the widows and orphans. You give warning to those who hurt them. And this widow is kind. I have seen her go out of her hut at night after putting her children to bed to bring her sick neighbors some groundnut soup. If any widow should have your help, God, it is this one!

But what about my own family? Will we be chased away too? I wouldn't mind so much if it was just me, but my family, God! My little ones! The special wife you gave me who is always kind to me. This is hard!

All night I have cried out to you. . . .

Oh, now I think I understand. The eyes in my heart are growing big like when I saw the great waterfalls the first time as a child. I understand now. . . Those who do what is right and protect others can stay in your village. I love your village, the one we live in on Sunday mornings when we dance and pray under the big tree. When we feel like you come to be with us.

I do not want to be chased away from that village, God! I must speak up for that widow today! Or blackness in my heart will chase me like a black leopard with hot yellow eyes that runs like a great wind in a storm and pounces on an animal to eat it!

Help me trust you! Give me the words for this widow today, so my heart—and our village—does not grow cold like a night where the light does not come.

I know! I will read today from the ancient book my father read to me so many times. I will read to the people about woe to those who take from widows. I will tell the people I warn them out of love for them. I will tell them what you have shown me this night about being chased away from the village of your peace.

I believe you will speak up for the widow too, God! You will come and put your arms inside the limbs of our big tree and whisper into our hearts like the rustling wind in the leaves. Then you will sing a soft, deep song that makes a good quiet in our souls. We will know you have spoken to us! Joy will explode in our hearts like a fish jumping up above the river in a sudden leap, or the leaves of some plants that grow so fast the children can practically stand and see them grow right before their very eyes! I know it now, God!

And I know if I speak your truth, others will feel like me too. Truth will flood their hearts like the waters of the river that swell in the spring rains. Many others will want more than anything, even life itself, to keep living in your village. Courage will grow in our hearts and eyes. And those who do not see your village in their hearts will be scared away by the light in the eyes of those who do!

I will walk with you today, God, to the funeral. I will not be alone. I will be big because of you. I feel your strength and joy in me now. I feel like the *mvula* tree when you come to be with us and spread yourself throughout its limbs.

PART II

SOLUTIONS

The next three chapters address possible solutions for widows. One examines the amazing stories of two women and how they overcame their circumstances. The next looks at how religion – so influential in Africa – can help or hurt. And the last looks at what we can all do.

GIRL IN
THE CONGO

8

TWO OF AFRICA'S FINEST

---

*"The biggest thing I have learned
is to love life as it is."*

A woman who was widowed young in the DR Congo

Of all the women I met in Africa, two stood out as lifting themselves up the most from the challenges of their lives. Neither is rich or famous. And, ironically, both are from the DR Congo, considered a "failed state." One is a widow and the other, the daughter of a widow. I met them both through the man on the elevator in Cape Town who said I must come to the Congo.

This chapter tells their amazing stories and looks at their keys to success. What caused them to have breakthroughs in their lives? What can be learned by other widows and their children from these two women? What can be learned from them by those who want to help widows? And what can all of us learn from their lives to apply to our own?

While both of these women live in the Congo, one was born in another Sub-Saharan country and the themes they describe culturally can apply to many parts of this region of the world. They have given permission for their stories to be shared in this book, but both have asked that I not use their real names or photos.

Therefore, I have given false names like so many in their country once colonized by French-speaking people. The photos you see are not of them but of situations similar to those they have described.

A WIDOW'S DAUGHTER

When I visited "Josephine" at her office in the Congo, she laid out for me a lovely lunch and her life story. Probably in her early 60s, she was one of the most spellbinding speakers I'd ever heard.

She'd had a great role model for inspirational speaking. When younger, she was assistant for four years to one of Africa's most respected men (his name has been withheld to help protect her identity). She now holds two Masters degrees and is in regional leadership for an international organization.

Josephine confirmed that the experiences of widows in the DR Congo are similar to what I'd heard in other African countries. "After a funeral, the widow comes back and all is gone. It happens everywhere," she said. "When you are talking about widows, you are talking about stories of loss.

"I myself was brought up by a widow who told me, 'My child, you will go to school. My children will go to school.'

"I cooked at four years of age, worked in the field at age six. My parents had worked in public administration. But when my dad died, my mother had to take the family back to my father's village. They didn't care for us. All they did was to take everything – the land, house, everything. You are told, 'You are a woman, you have no value.'"

Probably in her 60s, she was one of the most spellbinding speakers I'd ever heard.

But Josephine's mother worked hard and was one of the fortunate ones who found a way to put her daughter through school. "She would go and buy groundnuts and tell me to sit there by our house. 'Somebody will come and buy it,' she would say. She would put that hope in us. She would go to the field, she would come back, and we would have money. The next weekend the same thing would happen again."

I asked Josephine about the DRC's reputation as the rape capital of the world. "These men, the things they are doing, they did in the past too," she said. "When there is a crisis, the problem exacerbates. With the war, there is no control. No one will stop them.

"Women in the DRC are expected to be obedient," Josephine said, "even if their husbands beat them. Even if a husband beats you ten times, you are supposed to be quiet. 'Don't tell anybody,' they say. 'A good woman never tells stories of her home!' It is important for women to talk with other women about their problems. But women are discouraged from doing so, because then they are 'sharing secrets' of their home. But it is easier to do so with other women.

"Many people ask, 'Who is your father?' But sometimes the men become so violent that the children must flee. There are now many like this in the city center. There is still a lot of violence in the homes. And the children become fed up with the father."

"Does this go back many years in Africa?" I asked.

"Certainly. I was born. I found it. My mother was born. She found it. I hope our new generation will have access to certain information and skills so that they can live better than we did."

To sustain a job (for the few women who have them in the DRC), she explained, you must endure harassment. "If you have no training, you don't speak

Because she is educated, she says she can't be intimidated easily like other women.

up. But with training, the man says, 'Here I will not try.' Men say, 'These women who have gone to school are very dangerous.' They don't let their wives be friends with them.'"

Josephine now speaks seven languages. Because she is educated, she says she can't be intimidated easily like so many other women in her country. "Education exposure is key," she emphasized. So she encourages women to further their education. She told proudly of a woman she had influenced who was in her 50s and took a Master's in English abroad, graduating with distinction.

Josephine is designing a training program for Sunday schools in the churches for what is appropriate touch and what is not. "In the past," she said, "people were taught to keep quiet about such things." Given that a reported 80% of people in the DRC profess to be Christians,[1] such a program could have a major impact. She has also been asked to design a program to train 10,000 leaders and counselors for churches and church schools in the DRC. The purpose is so they can teach people about personal integrity and how to give dignity to every human being, whether male or female. She said that about 80% of the schools in the DRC are church schools, so that program could potentially reach many people in her country.

"The time has come for standing up," she said. "We must speak to the men, because they are the leaders. People say, 'But you are a woman. How can you talk to the men?' I say, 'God will help me.'"

A WIDOW

"Kenzy" looked to be in her late 30s – I found out later she was 54 – and seemed bright, intelligent, and warm. She presented herself tastefully in African dress, braided hair, and gold earrings. She was articulate and spoke English quite well, especially considering it was not her first language. She spoke with forthrightness and in the pleasant style and rhythms of English I've often heard in Sub-

PHOTO: MARK DARROUGH

Saharan Africa. "When my husband died, there was war in the Congo. He died during an attack in Katanga. He was 32.

"When we met, I was so young. We had three children. He was good to me. We did not have many problems. That was one of the things that sustained me [after he died].

"He was a teacher in a primary school. Then in our village where we live, they were recruiting soldiers. They were looking for strong men. They say you have done something bad. They put you in prison, to recruit you. They tell you to bring your wife. It is security for them if the man has a wife. You go where the man is training. You stay in a camp when they are in battle.

"My husband told me, 'Because I am a soldier, I don't know what day I will die. You have to study to care for the children. If you don't have a boy, my family will not help you.'

"My husband died during an attack in Katanga. I did not know for six months. I did not know where he was. Soldiers go several places. War was in several provinces, even when Mobutu was president.

177

They would say, 'Wives, you wait. He'll come back.' You don't know that he'll never come back.

"We [the soldiers' wives] were in a camp. They come and put something at your door to let you know your husband is not coming back. A knife, a piece of baggage. It is not even yours. But you find that. You start crying. Other women come to you.

"After, you go to the office. They tell you what they know. They give you the papers to tell you that you are a widow. But you never see the body.

"Then they say to you, 'You are a widow. You have to go back home.' They give you a small pension. It comes a while, then it stops. Or you have to journey to the province where you were to try to get it. You have to pay the ticket yourself. I left it because I lose a lot of time going back to get it and I had to leave my children.

"After his death I went back home to the family of my husband, because in our tradition when our husband go, you have to go back [to his] home with your children. You *have* to go back home. They will give you a house and someone to care for you.

"But I had only girls. I did not have a boy. So I could not have a house there. I had to stay in the home of my mother-in-law with my three daughters. I had to become like a servant to my mother-in-law. I did not have the right to have land or a field because of that, because girls don't inherit land. It was so difficult for me to stay there because of that.

I said I cannot go to be a second wife to somebody. They told me I was a bad woman.

"My husband's family wanted me to marry my brother-in-law, but I refused. They told me I was a bad woman. He had a wife. I said I cannot go to be a second wife to somebody.

"My girls could not go to school because they were girls. When you are 15 you have to be married. So it's not their concern to send them to school. But my husband told me, when I lose my life, in my family they don't care for girls. So I decided to go, to get work. They told me you cannot do that. You have to serve in your mother-in-law's home. I say, 'No, my children must go to school.' They say, 'If you don't stay here, we won't sustain you wherever you go.'

"What we had with my husband, they took everything. They say, 'Because you don't have a boy, you don't have the right to anything.' They took land, assets, even my clothes. So I went, I went with my three kids.

"I went to my family. But my family say the same: 'You've been married, you have children. You have to leave your children if you come to us.' I told them that my husband told me to care for my children, and I will do it to the end. I say I can do something to care for my children.

"I stayed in another village, where I could find a job. People said I was a prostitute because I was a woman who came from another town. It was not easy. Other men in the community were coming around me.

"Now people are starting to understand," she continued. "You have a right to say no [to a man's advances]. Our tradition is bad for the spread of HIV. People are beginning to understand that. Things are changing." Kenzy, still single, wears a wedding ring so men will not disturb her.

"I started going to the market, transporting something for people. I get some money, to get something for my children. To rent a small house. I was buying and selling fish. Maize, I sell. I go to work house cleaning. Sometimes I

It was very difficult to find a [regular] job, but I found one through a priest.

worked for food, or the [school] fees of my children. I did work at the school. That is what I did for 10 years.

"It was very difficult to find a [regular] job. But I found one through a priest. They had a health facility. I was a nurse, but even that was not enough. I was working nights. Two days of the week I did not work, so those days I did small, small work. I did that for 15 years. The other thing, God blessed me. I don't suffer illnesses, not much. I am strong. I don't have problems with health.

"My children are very intelligent in school, so some people pay fees. I would do books, clothes, food. After 10 years, my first girl finished secondary. Then my husband's brother, a teacher, paid for my girl to come here to university to study nursing and she married. The second one came here with her and she sent her to school.

"Then I came running here [to the capital] from the war. With these things of war, instability, I came here from eastern Congo [where the fighting was the worst]. My daughter and her husband told me to come.

"I know of many, many women who were murdered. So I do not want to go back. It is more peaceful now, in some areas. It is not war exactly. But they are still killing people. And someone may say, 'I have a problem with you. I don't want you to live with me.' So they engage people to kill you.

"One of my friends helped me to go back to school again. I did community health. At the end of that, I went back to school, to have a job to do only in the day and not the night.

ENCOURAGING OTHERS

"What I am doing now," Kenzy continued, "is we are going around the town to teach, to encourage women. Here in Congo a woman has not many considerations before a man. So I am fighting to empower women. So a young woman can look forward to something to do.

"If you are working, you can decide your life. A husband may be there, but you can have something to say, to contribute, to help decide the future of your children. You say no, my daughter will not marry [only]. She will go to school. But if you do not have a job, you cannot decide anything.

"I like being with women who don't have a lot, so we can share openly, discuss what they can do. Some go back to school, some find something to sell or something in the community to sustain the family.

"In our tradition, when a girl is a teenager, the parents prepare you to marry. Then that's it. They will not come to help you. You have to deal with your problems alone.

"So I tell small girls, 'You have the right to be prepared. You can do something for yourself. Decide for yourself! If you don't work, you cannot decide.'

"The big problem women have is they don't have opportunity to study. When you don't study, you can't go far. You cannot see far. You cannot think of being able to do something else. You cannot take risks. So you can fight [for a good life].

"A boy can go to Europe and study. But if a girl goes to school, it is a big battle. Families refuse, they cuss you. When I had that problem, I started praying. Because without that, I would not be able to resist [the pressure to stay in her husband's village, marry her brother-in-law, and keep her daughters home from school]. I was so young when my husband died, 28, with children. I am happy now because my children have grown. They work."

Kenzy now encourages women to find ways to keep their children in school. "When you are grown, if you don't have someone to sustain you, to encourage you, it's very difficult. Or you may be willing, but you don't have the means. But somebody may say, 'Tell the school you will pay small amounts.'

PHOTO: EDIFY.ORG

She also encourages the women themselves to go back to school. "So I go here and there, encouraging the women. Each time I am happy when I see a woman go to school. But if you become wife inheritance, they may say you are cursing our family [if you go to school].

"Living in town is sometimes good. You have several cultures. No one follows you. Everybody goes his way. But in the village it is very difficult. I could not stay in the village and say no to wife inheritance.

"Most of my work now, I do it with women in the churches. I speak with women who lack somebody to encourage them. When you encourage them, they are able to do many things. At the beginning, they say it is difficult to deal with. They are living in the situation. They say they have nothing they can do about it. Then you tell them your story. And they say, 'Ah!!' They realize they can do something about their situation too. They ask, 'What can *we* do?'

She now encourages women to find ways to keep their children in school.

"You have to be tired of your situation. I've been working with a group at a church for two years now. The church toilet had been broken a long time, and we needed $1,500 to replace it. After a year, we had only put $250 together. But we said, 'We have to continue this work!' So we decide to do a business to get enough for the toilet.

Then you tell them your story. And they say 'Ah!!' They ask, 'What can we do?'

"Then three went back to school. When they graduated, we had a big party. When the husband begins to see transformation in the woman, he encourages the woman to go back to school.

"We have many women here [in the capital] coming and going with the war. If she has the facility to talk about it, we listen. We pray. We take another appointment with the woman and she comes again. You listen to her. If she comes several times, she heals. She has shared her suffering.

"If she won't talk, you go several times to her. She may open up. Or you share your testimony. What we want is this woman to talk. When she talks, she can heal. When we meet again after that, we talk again about now. Here in town the women are the ones who care for the home. Women are mostly selling, doing small jobs, because of looking for food for the households.

"Most of the men have given up trying to find work. And in our tradition a man will care for the children of his sister, not his own. This is very, very difficult to deal with. The wife doesn't have the right to ask for money from her husband.

"And she must get permission from her husband for all she can do. When her husband has tradition in his head, the woman is like a thing. And she may have been traumatized several times with the war. Here in Kinshasa rape is not as much as in the East.

Most of the problem here is domestic violence. Women are beaten, abandoned. And abandonment is a big trauma, because she has the children and is alone.

Kenzy then made an interesting statement about widowhood I hadn't heard others in Africa state, especially given the shame heaped on widows, but perhaps they thought it. "Sometimes being a widow is better than being married. She is free for what she can think. She is free for what she can do."

"I have a young mother living in my home now. She tells me, 'My culture says...' But I am helping her to know and decide what to do with her life.

"I want to see women working, working! Even if somebody wants to put you down, he will be surprised to see you lifted up. He will say to himself, 'She is able to do this, so let us go together!'

"But one thing is true. Even when you are traumatized, God is there. He gives you what you need to survive. Encouragement is very important. You can lose all, but you can start again. You don't have to cry. Lift up! Lift up! I say, 'Never cry! Lift up! Challenge the challenge!'

"And the biggest thing I have learned is to love life as it is."

Kenzy now holds a Master's degree in Community Health, a remarkable feat, especially in a country like the Congo.

KEYS TO SUCCESS

What makes Josephine and Kenzy two of Africa's finest? Without a doubt, the common theme in their stories is education. In both lives, widowed mothers – Kenzy herself and Josephine's mother, though extremely disadvantaged economically, contended for their daughters to be educated.

Kenzy refused to marry her brother-in-law and live a life where her girls would not go to school, even though that was the culture in her husband's village. She had no financial resources

Kenzy worked two jobs for years to earn school fees for her children.

and jobs would be difficult to get. But she left there, found a job through a priest, and worked two jobs for years to earn school fees for her children.

Josephine's mother inspired her daughter to sell groundnuts successfully in front of their home, instilling faith in her daughter that people would buy them, and they did. This widow, reduced to working in the fields to feed her daughter instead of marriage to a government official, evidently did not turn bitter. Instead she kept a positive attitude and instilled that in her daughter. From these humble beginnings endued with the fine character of a widowed mother, Josephine eventually earned two Masters degrees and worked at the right hand of a world-famous leader.

Both Kenzy and Josephine were persistent to obtain advanced degrees. Both now encourage other women to be educated and celebrate their successes with them. And both were affected positively by men in religious positions. A Catholic priest helped Kenzy find a job, following the dictates of his faith to care for widows. Josephine learned from one of the world's great religious leaders, and in doing so became a fine leader herself.

Both women have been strong. Both refused to settle for mediocre lives. Both exercised courage and persistence in the pursuit of better lives, for themselves and others. Both are still doing so. These are lessons we can all learn from them.

WIDOWED YOUNG

Is that someone outside my door? It looks like the dark is still here. But are those the first peeks of day? Yes, I think morning is now coming. Almost time to rise.

Perhaps that sound is my friend's rooster. He makes us laugh sometimes. I hope it is just that rooster.

Nothing now. The sound is gone. I will rest a while longer here on the ground. Oh, Guillaume, how I miss you. I would not mind the ground with you beside me.

The girls are still asleep. I love them so. They comfort me while you are gone. Our girls. They bring us such joy. Even if girls aren't supposed to!

Well, I suppose it is time to rise now. I will get the best food in line if I go now. While I wait, I will let myself long for the time when you and I can go back to our home together, Guillaume.

What is that I see? Outside my door? A big broken dirty knife? Ayeeeeeeeeeee, I'd rather see a big black mamba snake than that! It can be killed. Have you been killed, Guillaume? No!!!!!!!!!

The other women are standing at the doors to their huts. They are all looking at me. With the look you give new widows. It must be true! Someone has gone around and told them!

Running, running, I must run to the lake! I cannot bear it here, their looks, this moment! Run, I must run! My children are still asleep. I pray they will stay that way. My friend Zawadi will watch them for me. I saw her look of a deep heart for me when the women stared. Some looked at me with hardness coming out of them. They are cold and mean. But Zawadi is not that way. She is my one true comfort here.

The guard sees me! He knows I am leaving the camp alone! He is staring at me! I know what he has done to many women in this camp. God, no! Make him go away! Is that a voice calling him? He is turning away now.

Run! I must run! My breath is panting in my chest like the

children when they are frightened and run home as fast as they can! The lake... I must get there... Maybe I will throw myself in, let my body go deep in the water! Find my man there? Go deeper than the well the missionaries put in when I was a child!

Here, here, I can rest at this rock by the lake. It is such a beautiful place. How can it still be beautiful when this news is so ugly?

Guillaume, Guillaume, are you really gone? I feel like my body is ripping in two.

Guillaume, you can't be gone! You came to me in a dream just a month ago... You said we would see each other again. You kissed me gently on my cheek... When I woke, the dream seemed so real. Like you were really with me... I felt your love on my cheek all day.

A broken knife! I cannot remember you like that... I don't want my children to remember you like that! They couldn't even leave a whole knife to tell me about you, Guillaume!

Your body! Where is your body? Did they bury it? Where are your beautiful bones? I want to wail over your beautiful body! I do not even have that! I hate this war! I hate it! Will it ever end?

A widow! I am a widow now! I am too young! Still in my 20s, my body full of life.

I must raise our girls alone now... No man in all of Congo will marry a woman with another man's children.

Yes, I can marry my husband's brother. He always looked at me when my husband was not there. With a bad smile and an evil look dancing in his eyes. I do not want a man like that!

Are you really gone, Guillaume? Ayeeeeeee! I feel my body shrinking. Like a breeze has stopped all of a sudden. I can no longer laugh with you at night. Oh, God, oh, God! Will I ever be happy again?

Orphans! My children are called orphans now because their father is gone! But I am living! Even if people think a mama is not important.

The land! The land too! The land is no longer mine with you! I cared for it too. Your land, Guillaume...where we first lived. Where I worked the earth to grow food for us. Where I became full with our children. Where I laughed as my belly grew large as a big pumpkin. Leaning over to pull weeds became hard then. But I didn't care! I was so happy to have our first child inside me.

A boy or a girl? I kept thinking about that. Most people wanted boys. But I wanted a girl. I never told you that. I wanted a girl to play with like a sister. To laugh at the things girls laugh at together. To hold my hand and stroke my head when I was old and dying. To give me a cup of cool water. To bathe my body after it slipped away to meet my God, to dance there in the big festivals of heaven.

Our land! For I came to think of it so. Where I had the first birthing with our oldest girl. Where our second daughter was born. She came so quickly while I was in the fields. We buried her birth sac there. How can I leave that land? It has a piece of my body and heart!

Now your family will take back that land. Woman, they will say, it was never yours. It belongs to the men.

How will I get food for our girls now? Now that I have no land to grow it on? What will some people want me to do for food?

You are nothing, people will say! Nothing without a man! Marry your husband's brother to care for you and your daughters. You will be lucky to get food from that. Give your body to him whenever he wants you! Take the bad treatment from his first wife and her children and his mother. At least you and your children will eat! Unless you want to become one of those women who lets any man come into her hut just to get a cup of maize for her children.

God! I cannot do those things! Please show me another way!

Guillaume, I promise you! I will care for our girls! Even though people say I am just a woman. Even though I am now a widow. Oh... I promise you, Guillaume! I promise you, world! I will send them to school! Even though people say girls are not important! I will send them to school. Somehow I will find a way! God, please help me find a way!

A widow! Oh, God! I am a widow now! A young widow! A young widow with three daughters! Help me to give them a good life!

... Then, her first burst of grief and shock spent for the moment, she turned and headed back to the camp and her children.

*WORSHIP
IN BURUNDI*

9

RELIGION: HELPING OR HURTING?

The issue of widows
"Needs a revolution...
Whatever it takes is worth
the sacrifice. "[1]

Augustine Okwunna Odimmegwa, Nigerian Catholic priest

Africans say they are "notoriously religious" and that culture and religion embrace all areas of their lives.[2] So a look at widows in Africa would not be complete without considering how religion is helping, or hurting, them. We saw a few examples in the Zambia chapter, but what is the picture overall? And can religion help bring the breakthrough that is so needed by Africa's widows?

A strong majority of people in Sub-Saharan Africa profess Christianity.[3] For example, more than 80% of people in six of the seven African countries I visited say it is their religion.[4] About three-fourths say they attend services at least once a week, usually in their finest garb, enjoying vibrant African worship music.[5] About half of Christians in this region are Catholic.[6]

Islam is predominant mainly in northern Africa, though it does have many followers in Sub-Saharan Africa, especially in the northern part of it closest to North Africa. Many people of both faiths, however, incorporate traditional African religion into their lives.[7] Practices include sacrifices to ancestors and spirits to protect them from harm, and widowhood rituals. In Tanzania, a recent study found that 78% of Christians believe in spells and curses.[8]

My research did not focus on Muslim widows, and this religion is not the majority in Sub-Saharan Africa, so I will leave a discussion of it to others, except for two general comments. First, the United Nations has concluded that, regardless of religion, it is common for widows in Sub-Saharan Africa to be chased off their homes.[9] Second, a Kenyan academic cites relevant research into land rights, which so dramatically affect widows: "In principle, Islam grants women greater land rights than customary [traditional] law. However, in practice, these rights are generally not respected."[10]

With the high percentage of Christians in Sub-Saharan Africa, the strong biblical call to help widows, and the continued practice of African traditional religion by many, what impact is Christianity actually having on African widows?

As we look at that question, I should say that I grew up in the Christian church. Eventually I became disillusioned, left it as a young woman, and then returned in my thirties to reclaim the deep faith experiences of my childhood. Eventually I organized large Christian events with tens of thousands of people and had the privilege of opening in prayer for Billy Graham at our local stadium in front of 46,000 people.

I have taught on the biblical passages on women in leadership, citing theologians who affirm the full partnership of women in ministry, and my work on that topic has been published by a respected organization.[11] I was also on the leadership team for five years for the international Lausanne Movement, one of the world's most respected Christian organizations, which produced "the most representative gathering of Christians ever held."[12]

My faith remains. But I've seen some of the best and worst of Christianity in practice. Many Africans, I'm sure, can say that too. Some of them have spoken out powerfully about the disappointing treatment of widows by the church.

Esther Mombo, dean of a university in Kenya, tells of a widow being forced into "widow cleansing" – the custom of having sex with another man to "break her spiritual tie" with her dead husband. "I screamed!" the widow said. "I told the pastor they are forcing me to do this!" But her pastor did nothing to prevent it, saying 'That is our culture.'"[13]

A Nigerian Catholic priest, Augustine Odimmegwa, did his doctoral work on widows, the only African man I know of to do so. He says only God knows how many widows have "lost their faith in God and humanity" because of what they have suffered at the hands of their in-laws and society.[14] This is particularly true, he says, when they go to church together. Another African priest says the church's silence on widows has contributed to the "unchecked, socially inflicted atrocities" on them through the years.[15]

Some priests and church members, however, have suffered "untold disgrace, emotional trauma, and all kinds of humiliation" fighting for the cause of widows.[16] Records show that in 1939, several Catholic and Anglican churches in Nigeria worked together to try to end the custom of a widow without a male child receiving no inheritance. But the traditional chief in the area rejected the idea.[17] More recently, a brave priest resolved that anyone who made a Christian widow go the local pagan priest for "sexual cleansing" after the husband's death would be excluded from his church.[18]

'I screamed!' the widow said. 'I told the pastor they are forcing me to do this!'

Some Catholic women organizations have also called for more humane treatment of widows, such as ritual hair shaving by sympathetic friends rather than angry relatives of the deceased husband.[19] The Pan African Christian Women Assembly called in 1994 for churches to protect widows and their property.[20]

Patricia Okoye, who holds a doctorate in education, is the most in-depth author on widowhood rituals I have discovered. She says that as communities have turned Christian, they have changed many of the harmful widowhood practices. In fact, she believes that Christianity poses the strongest force to bring change to widowhood practices in her country.[21]

Why would Christianity have such an impact on the treatment of widows? Because many strong passages in the Bible talk specifically about the treatment of widows. We saw some of these in the last chapter and the box lists more. These passages say God protects widows, that harm will come to those who hurt widows, and that caring for widows is considered "true religion" and brings a blessing.

CULTURAL SHIFT NEEDED

These strong passages, though, have not been enough, in one of the most Christian areas of the world, to effect widespread change regarding widows' suffering. Why? Certainly, the verses need to be taught more in churches and at funerals, as we saw some pastors doing in the last chapter. But if we get at contributing causes discussed at the beginning of this book, then Christianity in Africa, and beyond, also needs to address how women are treated as a gender. Unfortunately, the poor experiences of many widows reflect the larger treatment of women in general.

Victor Nakah was a seminary president for 10 years in Zimbabwe and has traveled across Africa for his work with more than 100 seminaries. He is a big, winsome man, and a natural leader.

THE BIBLE ON WIDOWS...

DO NOT HARM

Cursed is anyone who withholds justice from the... widow.[22]

Woe to those who make... widows their prey.[23]

You sent widows away empty-handed and broke the strength of the fatherless. That is why snares are all around you, why sudden peril terrifies you...[24]

GOD DEFENDS

For the Lord your God... defends the cause of the fatherless and the widow.[25]

The LORD tears down the house of the proud but he keeps the widow's boundaries intact.[26]

I [God] will be quick to testify against... those... who oppress the widows and the fatherless.[27]

CARE FOR THEM

Religion that God our Father accepts as pure and faultless is this: to look after orphans and widows in their distress...[28]

Defend the cause of the fatherless, plead the case of the widow.[29]

You shall give [a tenth of all your produce every three years] to the Levite, the alien, the fatherless and the widow, so that they may eat.[30] So that the LORD your God may bless you in all the works of your hands.[31]

More biblical passages about widows, grabbing land or goods, helping the poor, and justice are listed in the endnote.[32]

"The church in Africa is very influential," Victor told me, "and growing fast. The church is influential to the point that if it begins to role model good marriage relationships and the treatment of widows, then it will have an impact on society in general. But we're not doing a good job of male-female relationships. We have failed God in how we have treated our wives and sisters.

Reverend Victor Nakah, Th.D.

"We need wholesome relationships of respect, mutual support, and complementing one another. We need to disciple the Christian men who still act like traditional culture. So you realize the old way is unbiblical, un-Christian. It's a clash of worldviews. So you think, 'Maybe I need to talk to my wife, say how really sorry I am at how I've treated you, looked at you.'

"Change should start in the church, with men repenting of their wrong attitudes toward women, their unbiblical, un-Christian understanding of women and their role. Yes, there are issues that are very debatable. But 'headship' [a teaching some follow that the man is the head of the home] is not superiority. It is a headship of servanthood. Submission does not mean inferiority. Scripture is very clear that men and women are equal.

"We have to think differently about marriage roles. We have to allow God's word to beam on culture. Then you can see all the negative things in the culture. It's a paradigm shift. And it's practical. It's how you treat your family, how you look at your wife.

"Every morning," Victor said, "I wake up and ask the Lord, 'How can I serve my dear wife today?' Then I do silly little things. She's a librarian at the seminary and takes tea at 11 a.m. I now work from home, so sometimes I'll call her at 10:30 a.m. and ask if I can bring her tea."

Then a woman can stand up to a man who is putting her down with abuse or beatings.

At that point I exclaimed, "And I bet you have a happy wife!" Victor, this huge wise man who is a leader in Africa and obviously has a good marriage, answered with a big smile: "I love having a happy wife! I *run* home to a happy wife!"

After that, I wanted to speak with Victor's wife! She also stressed the importance of Christianity's impact and its potential to bring change for widows.[33]

"When you grow up in tradition," Nosizo said, "you see what happens to your mother and you follow that, but education can change your view. And being a Christian works on your self-esteem. It helps you to become who you are – who you are in Christ, to be happy in who you are, and what you can do in Christ. Then a woman can stand up to a man who is putting her down with emotional abuse or beatings.

"Laws to protect women [including inheritance for widows] are important," she continued. "But what we believe influences us. If culture still influences us, we can run into a lot of problems. There are a lot of things we've not allowed Christ into. We need to get to the point where he influences all. God is able. The more we allow what we learn from Scriptures to influence us, it's possible. Culture is the key. And only God can change that."

TRADITIONAL AFRICAN RELIGION

Patricia Okoye, who wrote the most definitive book I have found on widowhood rituals, says cultural practices of traditional African religion are a great obstacle in the way of change for widows.

As we have seen, this worldview often holds that a widow must perform dehumanizing rites to ensure her husband's entry into a good afterlife, prevent curses to her family and community, and prove her innocence in his death. Different forms of traditional African religion are practiced across Africa, but many similarities exist, especially when it comes to widows.

If a widow does not perform these rites, she may contribute to the rejection of her dead husband "into the bosom of his forebears," Okoye says, which is considered an "abomination, a sacrilege."[34] Epidemics, diseases, famine, pestilence, and even deaths of extended family members may result.[35] "It is better imagined than experienced," she claims, "the kind of vengeance that society visits on an erring widow."[36]

Traditional African religion, as practiced in some places, also holds that someone is responsible for every death, that none are from natural causes. So even if the widow performs all the rites to appease her dead husband's spirit and attempt to prove her innocence, she may still be blamed for her husband's death. In such a case, she could receive punishment "equal to that given to a convicted murderer."[37] In fact, Okoye says, death may be "the final stage of punishment meted out to offenders for any manner of religious transgressions."[38]

As stated earlier, Okoye sees Christianity with the greatest potential to change this deeply entrenched worldview.[39] Father Odimmegwa agrees. He calls for teaching on how Christianity is a convincing alternative to aspects of traditional African religion that are degrading to widows.[40] How would such teaching work? He does not develop that train of thought in his doctoral work, and I could not locate a study by an African theologian on this topic as related to widows. So I will

Even if a widow performs all the rites, she may still be blamed for her husband's death.

propose a few thoughts here and hope that an African theologian will address them further.

Basic tenets of Christianity and many forms of traditional African beliefs share some similarities, so could these expand the African world view, rather than eliminate it, in ways that would be helpful to widows? For example, Christianity agrees with many forms of traditional African religion that blood sacrifice is indeed necessary to atone for sin. But instead of putting a widow through tormenting rites, or even taking her life in order to appease the dead husband, Christianity teaches that the blood of Jesus was shed once and for all as a sacrifice to pay the price for human sin.

Traditional African religion claims that newly departed spirits can hover and cause trouble for the family and village unless certain rites are performed by a widow. Christianity also teaches that spiritual life continues after an earthly life, and that demons can harass humans. But Christianity teaches that demons can be cast away and curses broken by praying in faith in the name of Jesus.

Traditional African religion tends to see men as in charge and may justify men taking possessions from widows and casting them out, thereby getting a blessing of material value. Kenyan David Kodia, principal of a college there, says the word of God can show how to access the blessings of God, and this would be in ways that do not harm others.[41] Kodia also says the church must be careful with the selective application of passages of the Bible and conservative theories that legitimize inappropriate male dominance, which is so prevalent in many forms of traditional African religion and the culture in general.

MALE DOMINANCE?

What are these biblical passages that are sometimes used to legitimize male dominance? There are just a few, but a surface reading does not give an accurate understanding. They must be

199

examined in depth, considering the original language used and the cultural context. These debated passages have been used inaccurately for centuries to justify male abuse of women. If they are misunderstood and taught across Africa (and elsewhere) to justify inappropriate male dominance, they will reinforce the entrenched cultural concepts discussed in chapter one, with man as the "god" in the home. Then Christianity will be used to hurt women and widows further, which is a travesty.

First is the concept of the "headship" of men over women, that men are in charge of women. When Victor Nakah referred to this idea, he said it is debatable. In fact, Bible scholars hotly debate the interpretation and translation of the verses used to build this theory.[42] The main passage used for it draws on a biblical verse stating that man is the "head" of woman, but the word for "head" in the original language, Greek, can mean either "authority" or "source."[43] One must examine the context of the passage to select the meaning. The theme of "source" is stated explicitly in the passage: men and women came from each other, they are not independent of each other, and everything comes from God.[44] Regardless of how one interprets this passage, however, any "headship," as Victor Nakah wisely stated, is to be one of servanthood, a theme Jesus emphasized.[45]

The second Bible passage used to justify male dominance states that a woman should not teach or have authority over a man.[46] The word used here for "authority," however, is not the usual Greek word for this concept.[47] In fact, this particular word appears only this once in the Bible, and its meaning is also one of the most highly debated by scholars. Much research indicates that the word means exercising an inappropriate and heavy-handed type of authority. Paul was writing this passage to Ephesus, where belief in the goddess Diana permeated the culture and it was taught that women were superior to men. Therefore some scholars believe he may have been correcting pagan misunderstandings popular there and not allowing women to teach such beliefs of their superiority as a gender in the church.⁴⁸ Some people also use a passage about men as church overseers and elders to justify inappropriate male dominance.⁴⁹ However, there is much debate among scholars about the scriptural passages on this issue too, and even some instances of blatant translator bias.

We do know that women were leaders in the early church, with Phoebe, for example, described with the same title as Paul, a minister of the gospel.⁵⁰ Junia was called an apostle, a highly esteemed position.⁵¹ Even the fourth-century bishop of Constantinople, Chrysostom, referred to her as a woman "counted worthy of the appellation of apostle."⁵²

The last passage commonly used to justify male dominance is the one that says a woman is to "submit" to her husband.⁵³ In the verse right before, however, the author calls for *mutual submission* as an overarching principle. In fact, when Paul says a wife should submit to her husband, the verb for "submit" is missing in the original language. Instead, what appears is a series of three dots called an "ellipsis" in the Greek, indicating one goes back to the prior verb. This verb appears in the preceding sentence about mutual submission, reinforcing that overarching principle.

Tellingly, in the same passage, a husband is taught to love his wife as Christ loved the church and gave himself up for her, a radical concept in a time when women had few rights in society.⁵⁴ Perhaps most sobering for a husband, he is taught to love and treat his wife with respect, or his prayers will be hindered.⁵⁵ And in Christianity in general, followers are taught to love one another, prefer one another, serve one another.⁵⁶

It should be stated emphatically that the Bible never condones physical abuse in a marriage. If Christian Scripture is used to justify such, that adds spiritual abuse, implying falsely that God himself endorses such behavior. Esther Mombo of Kenya contends that churches need to teach that all forms of violence in marriage, so prevalent in Africa and around the world, are a sin.[57] A major document produced by the world's largest gathering of Christians, including many Africans, to date – the Lausanne Congress held in Cape Town, South Africa, agrees:

> **"We deny that any cultural custom or distorted biblical interpretation can justify the beating of a wife. We grieve that it is found among professing Christians, including pastors and leaders. We have no hesitation in denouncing it as a sin."**
>
> *– The Cape Town Commitment* [58]

Furthermore, the Bible never gives instructions for a wife to "obey" her husband, as it does for children to parents. The word used for wives is "submit," meaning to cooperate voluntarily. It does not mean blind obedience no matter what and is in the context of mutual submission. Numerous other passages also confirm this mutuality in marriage.[59]

Pope John Paul II wrote on the importance of mutual submission in marriage. He said that when the equality of husband and wife is violated, it is not good for the woman, but it "also diminishes the true dignity of the man."[60] Mutual submission and serving others willingly take spiritual maturity. But without them, in marriage and in life, one has missed the heart of Christian teachings, and the blessings that come from them.

One other relevant passage bears mention. When God created woman, some Bible translations say, she was a "helper." [61] But a recognized Old Testament scholar and long-time president of a highly respected seminary, points out that the word for "helper"

When the equality of husband and wife is violated, it diminishes the man's dignity.

is a word used many times in the Old Testament to describe the strength God himself brings.[62] A more accurate translation of the phrase about woman, he says, is "a power or strength corresponding to the man."[63]

Adam and Eve were given dominion over the earth together.[64] It was not given to man alone. Then sin brought God's prediction, not a curse, as multiple respected scholars have concluded after study, that men would rule over women.[65] From a Christian viewpoint, though, Jesus died to atone for sin, freedom from curses, and restoration back to God's original design.

So, a deeper study of the controversial passages indicates that a woman can be seen as a powerful partner for a better life, not someone inferior to act as a slave. The Bible clearly indicates greater blessings come, for both men and women, from living a life that treats both sexes with respect and dignity. This, rather than worldly concepts of domination and submission, is what empowers men and women to fulfill their God-given destinies.

For Africans who want to examine the above Scriptures in more depth, studies have been translated by a Kenyan pastor, the Reverend Philip Owasi, into Swahili, spoken by approximately 100 million people in Africa.[66] Another excellent resource, co-written by the founder of one of the world's largest Christian mission agencies, is available in French for the many Francophone Africans, as well as English and a dozen other languages.[67]

Whatever one's viewpoint on the standing of women in the church and in marriage, though, if women are treated with the respect and equality before God that is described in the Bible, then the lives of many women and widows, as well as many men, will surely change for the better.

JESUS, WOMEN, AND WIDOWS

If there is any doubt for a Christian on how women and widows should be treated, then the model of Jesus himself sheds further light. When Jesus was born, women were seen as inferior to men, as they are in much of Africa and many other places around the world today. The Rome-conquered Jews of Jesus' time were influenced by Greek thought against women. After the leadership of outstanding women in the Old Testament, for the first time Jewish writings demeaned women. It was considered shameful for women to study the Torah – the Jewish Scripture, and a rabbi was not even to converse with a Jewish woman he did not know in public.[68] But Jesus did not bend to that culture.

He taught women – when Mary "sat at his feet" that was a well-known phrase then meaning to be a student.[69] He interacted with them – his conversation about spiritual matters with the Samaritan woman at the well is the longest recorded in the Bible.[70] He appeared first to women after he rose from the grave – commissioning them first to share the news that he was risen. He rebuked his disciples when they did not believe the women – in a time when women's testimony was not considered reliable in a court of law.[71]

One day a woman cried out to Jesus that his mother was blessed to have given birth to him, which was the measure of a woman's worth in that day – especially with sons, as in many places in Africa today. Jesus replied to this woman that blessed rather are those who hear the word of God and obey it.[72] So Jesus gave women a broader worth than only childbirth – a spiritual one.

The Bible records that Jesus only chose twelve male disciples – but he selected them to go to Jewish believers, and they would not have allowed women to speak to their assemblies. It was radical enough for that time that Jesus included women in his followers, and that they traveled with him and even supported him financially.[73]

After Jesus' ascension, women were a key part of the launch of his church. Women were in the group of 120 believers who gathered together in prayer, waiting for the power Jesus said would "come upon" them.[74] All were filled with the Holy Spirit and began speaking in other tongues (languages) they did not know.[75] Peter, one of the apostles, told the crowd that this was what the prophet Joel had said, that both sons and daughters would prophesy.[76] From there, women were leaders in the early church and Paul's co-workers in the work of the gospel, as he affirmed in various passages.[77]

PHOTO: JOHN CREWS

And what of Jesus and widows? A widow named Anna prophesied over him when he was brought to the temple as a baby to be dedicated.[78] When he hung on a cross, he tenderly put his mother, probably then a widow, and his beloved disciple John into one another's care as mother and son.[79] He raised the son of a widow from the dead.[80] He used as a role model the example of a persistent widow who kept coming to a judge for justice and finally got it.[81]

When Jesus was teaching in the temple courts, he talked about widows. He said to watch out for teachers of the (religious) law who devour widows' houses and would be punished severely. He saw a poor widow give to two small coins to the temple, called his disciples to him, and told them this poor widow had put more into the treasury than all the others, for it was all she had to live on. Was Jesus happy about this, or sad? The Bible does not say. But if one looks at the passage in context, it is not about sacrificial giving. Rather, it was about teachers of the law devouring widow's houses.[82] Perhaps Jesus was grieved and angry that widows were pressured to give all they had, rather than being cared for by a loving church, as happened after his resurrection.[83]

When Jesus was teaching in the temple courts, he talked about widows.

In the new Christian church, widows were helped and certain guidelines applied. A widow had to be really in need, not have family who could care for them, over 60, known for good deeds and faithfulness to her husband when he lived, and someone who continued night and day to ask God for help. Younger widows were encouraged in the early church to remarry.[84] Are these guidelines realistic in Africa today?

As we have seen, most widows in Sub-Saharan Africa do not remarry. The exception is to a brother-in-law as a multiple wife. Perhaps polygamy and "levirate" marriage (to a deceased husband's male relative) are merciful accommodations to make the best of a bad situation if a widow has no other options. But these cannot be seen, from the creation account in Genesis, the teachings of Jesus,[85] or the accounts from widows themselves, to be God's best plan.

While multitudes of widows in Africa do have family, many of their families are so poor that caring properly for a widow, especially with young children, is not realistic, and widows often cannot find decent jobs. So the above guidelines from the New Testament would not comply with a foundational Christian principle of caring for the poor and needy.

Can the church in Africa care for all the needy widows? Not likely, given the vast numbers of widows and poor in Africa. Is this justification for not caring for any widows? I think not. But there are additional things churches can do not requiring material assistance.

CALL FOR A REVOLUTION

Father Odimmegwa, the priest who did his doctoral research on widows, says the church has a divine responsibility to fight for them. He has called urgently for the plight of widows to be included in the social justice agenda of the Catholic Church. The issue needs a "revolution," he says, and "whatever it takes is worth the sacrifice."[86]

He has made strong, practical recommendations for churches to help widows. These include:

...preaching about the evils of widowhood customs,

...working with traditional rulers and chiefs to agree on a pastoral approach to widows,

...teaching Christianity as an acceptable alternative to age-long widowhood rituals,

...teaching on the equality of male and female,

...using the prestige of the church to influence political and civic leaders,

...encouraging women's groups to stop injustices with widows,

...censuring church members who mistreat widows,

...establishing widows' associations,

...helping widows in practical ways, and

...establishing an annual event to focus on widows.[87]

Perhaps the annual event could take place around June 23, International Widows' Day.

Victor Nakah, the former seminary president, agrees that churches should use their political influence to help widows. "The church needs to lobby its legislators and politicians to change laws. If 150 churches push on the same issue, it's powerful, but often the churches don't speak out." A recent study by two Nigerian women academics underscores why this is so important. The authors found that religious leaders had a significant influence on a campaign to change laws to lessen the mistreatment of widows.[88] "We have women's organizations and all that," says Victor, "but men in the church should fight for our mothers, our sisters, and our grandmothers."

Gideon Para-Mallam of Nigeria, a regional leader across numerous African countries for an international religious

Men in the church should fight for our mothers, our sisters, and our grandmothers.

organization, agrees. "I think the church needs to incorporate the plight of widows and orphans into its agenda," he told me. "It is not enough just to pay lip service to the plight of widows. Something needs to be done in a sustainable way with holistic care-giving for widows. And the best support is what a fellow widow could bring or give to other widows. We need to be intentional in connecting widows across churches and denominations and nations."

Churches in the West also need to partner with African churches and NGOs for the gargantuan task of helping the widows of Sub-Saharan Africa, estimated at one quarter of women there. One of the largest churches in the U.S., Saddleback Church in California, has done just that. It has sent attorneys who have trained over 200 pastors in Rwanda on how to prevent property grabbing from widows.[89]

If every church, no matter how large or small, no matter where in the world, could find a way to help at least one African widow, it would make a huge difference. A United Nations publication said there is no group more affected by the "sin of omission" than widows.[90] Is the church listening?

A BRIGHT LIGHT

The old man slept. He was close to the end of his life. He knew, and his family knew.

Then he awakened. The light was so bright where he slept he wondered if the whole world was on fire. A huge being stood over him. His frail old bones cowered back on the mat that held his thin body. All at once he felt the greatest fear and greatest peace he had ever known. Then it spoke. "Fear not. I am here to help you. Give your cloak to the widow who sits naked on the cold ashes mourning her husband."

Then it was gone! The old man blinked and turned his body a bit to test it. He felt his usual pains. Yes, I am still alive, he thought. The hut looked the same. But the old man knew what he had just experienced was real, more real than the frayed mat he lay on.

He felt sadness for the first time at how he had treated widows all his life. How he had taken the land and pots and pans from his brother's widow? She had been so kind to me, he thought. How could I do that?

All of a sudden his great-grandson came to him. He was only eleven but he a special boy.

"Bibi, are you good? I woke up just now thinking to check on you. That was so big in my head I had to come right away."

"Ah, my young one, you are a good one, a wise one. Your life will be great. But now I must take my old wrap, my *kitenge*, to the widow who has sat for days on the cold ashes mourning her husband."

"Bibi, please do not do this. You will die without your *kitenge*. The nights are cool from the big rains. Your body will shake with cold. We do not have another one to give you. Please, Bibi, do not do this. You will grow weaker. My heart will be cold if you leave this earth."

The old man told the young boy his dream. The boy listened with wide eyes while the old man spoke. The boy

209

could almost see the fiery being from hearing about it. His heart felt big inside him. The old man glowed with happiness and awe as he spoke. The boy had never seen this from the man he had known all his life.

Then the old man pulled the *kitenge* off his body, leaving it naked. He began to push himself up to take his wrap to the widow.

"Wait, Bibi, I will take the *kitenge* for you to the widow! Stay here and rest! I will even tell her of your dream. "

Then the old man held out the *kitenge* to the boy and collapsed back onto his mat.

"He saw what?" the widow asked the boy again. Joy had spread over her face like a spring rising from dry earth. The boy told her once again, quickly, because he wanted to get back to his old Bibi.

Suddenly, the widow wrapped the *kitenge* around her nakedness, wiping the ashes from her as best she could. "I must thank him!" she said. She remembered well how the old man had tormented her own widowed mother. So the gift of the threadbare cloth was extra sweet. No piece of cloth she had ever worn was as beautiful to her. The villagers might give her a beating for leaving her widow's ashes, but she did not care.

Together the young widow and the boy ran like happy wind through the village. When they entered the hut, the first gleam of dawn was entering it where the old man lay. It draped across his face, lighting it up. But he was clearly now dead and had a smile of peace neither she nor the boy had ever seen on him.

Together, the special boy of eleven years and the young widow turned to tell the village of the wonders that had visited them that night.

MARIE CHANTAL:
20-YEAR OLD WIDOW
WITH TWINS

10

A WHOLE PIECE
OF CLOTH

---

*"Today I feel free. I can share my story
without crying."*

Glegonie, a widow in Burundi

Who will help Africa's widows? Who will share half a piece of cloth with widows as Aunty Margaret's friend did in Ghana? And what does it take for widows to have a whole piece of cloth, a full and satisfying life?

Throughout this book we have met many courageous widows, like:

...Phelomena in Rwanda, who ran from the genocide with a baby on her back.
...Faustina in Ghana, who sells sandals from a basket, trying to keep her land from her in-laws.
...Dorothy in a refugee camp in Uganda, who fought for her land and was stabbed with a knife.
...Niane in a South African township, who calls the police repeatedly for an abused neighbor.
...Beatrice in the Congo, who sews clothes in a dangerous market to feed her children.

...Matilda in Zambia, who learned her rights and kept her land from greedy in-laws.

We've seen how widows in multiple countries are blamed for the husband's death, stripped of assets, possibly subjected to dehumanizing widowhood rituals, and left desperate with their children, without welfare or other safety nets. We've learned the problem is huge, with one in four women in Sub-Saharan Africa estimated to be a widow, many of them young with small children, and destitute.

We've looked at underlying causes and seen how HIV/AIDS and wars have multiplied the number of widows, as well as those blamed for deaths by traditional African religion. We've seen how some laws specify protections for widows, but that these may not be effective in the villages, the majority of Sub-Saharan Africa. We've seen the potential for Christianity to bring change, with its many biblical passages about helping and protecting widows, caring for one another, and treating women and wives with respect.

We've also seen how critical education is to change the lives of widows and their children. Throughout my travels, many widows lamented that they couldn't pay school fees for their children. Even the "free" public schools generally require payment of certain fees, and without a school certificate, their children won't be able to get decent jobs when grown. Aunty Margaret in Ghana said she cried every day because she couldn't pay her 17-year-old son's fees. Widows in the Uganda camp for displaced persons almost all mentioned needing school fees. Claudine, the widow's daughter in Rwanda, wept when she said she didn't even have money as a girl for pencils to go to school.

We've heard the cry for economic empowerment arise from widows in the countries of Sub-Saharan Africa I visited. Faustina sells sandals from a basket in Ghana, even though she seems quite intelligent to me. Aunty Margaret, also very intelligent, said it was impossible for her to get a job other than helping someone in the market just to get something to eat. The professional women in the DR Congo said banks won't trust widows to give them business loans. Bishop Banda in Zambia summed it up by saying that the most important thing is to empower widows economically.

We've also met heroes, both individuals and some groups, who fight for widows. Like Ken Oketta in Uganda who developed the document about cultural care for widows with tribal leaders, and Bishop Banda in Zambia who advocates spiritually and practically for widows, and International Justice Mission, which fights for widows' rights legally in multiple African countries.

Other heroes include multiple groups who have fought for land rights for women in Africa,[1] widows' organizations large and small, and even some African novelists who have written about widows to challenge their treatment culturally. I highly recommend three in particular. One of them is listed in the top 100 African books of the century. (The three books are described in the endnote.[2])

Two champions for widows have fought for them globally. One is Raj Loomba, a Pakistani businessman living in London. When he was being married as a young man, the priest at his wedding asked his widowed mother to stand away from the couple so she would not bring them bad luck. This haunted him and eventually he established International Widows Day in London. He then successfully lobbied the United Nations to declare such a day starting in 2011.[3] A growing annual observance, it has begun to help the cause of the estimated 245 million widows worldwide.[4] It occurs on June 23, the day Raj Loomba's mother was widowed.

Margaret Owen, a Cambridge-educated barrister now in her 80s, has championed widows globally for 20 years. Her work began when a woman from Malawi visited her and expressed astonishment that her in-laws allowed her to keep her home after her husband died. So Owen wrote *A World of Widows* in 1995. It takes a global view of widows, especially in Asia and Africa, and she has advocated for widows ever since.[5]

BURUNDI WIDOWS TRANSFORMING

Another hero for widows at the grassroots level is Peace Nihorimbere, who is helping to bring wholeness to the lives of widows in her native Burundi. I did not find many programs solely for widows when I traveled in Africa, so hers stands out.

Burundi is beautiful and broken, says a friend who lives there. Lake Tanganyika, with white sand beaches, is so large one can't see its end. But that white sand ran red with the blood of war not so long ago, with fighting until a 2005 ceasefire. Burundi and Rwanda were once one country, and they have the same ethnic issues. Burundi's war is not as well as known as Rwanda's, though. Mass slaughter did not happen in a terrible 90 days as it did in Rwanda. Burundi's civil war went on for 12 years, with an estimated 200,000 people killed and hundreds of thousands displaced from their homes.[6]

Unlike Rwanda, Burundi has been largely neglected by the international community, though that is beginning to change, and it is one of the world's most malnourished countries. Its many widows, some from the fighting, are often young with children, destitute, and hungry.

Peace and her staff teach the widows how to sew in a one-year program so they have a skill to support themselves and their children. They also love the widows to wholeness day by day. The training is a complete gift for the widows, who often do not have resources for a daily meal, much less for such a training program.

When I first visited Peace's program, it had a vibrant group of young women. But only two of the 22 women were widows. I interviewed those two widows, as well as two who had previously taken Peace's one-year class.

The widows who had completed the course radiated confidence in colorful African attire they'd made that set off their features and personalities. The first was Sylvie, a dynamic young woman in red, age 39. She told me she'd had two husbands murdered, one right in front of her during the war. She was the mother of five children, two of whom had died, and she had prayed desperately that God would help her. Then she heard at church about a place where she could learn skills – Peace's program.

"When I came here," she told me through a translator, "I found parents, people who treated us like parents would. They paid transport. They cared about us in all situations – health treatment, medicines. They cared. They even gave us a [sewing] machine."

Another widow, Glegonie, age 38, grew up an "orphan," as she said, with only a mother. "After the death of my husband, it was very difficult. In my family no one cared about me, and I was living a life of weeping and tears. I was discouraged, saying my life was at an end. No one was standing by me to encourage me. My oldest child was four, the second was two years. After I gave birth to a third, I had not even something to eat.

"But once I came here, I started to learn, I started to feel joy. They teach us God's word to comfort us. They teach us how to face situations. I used to hear many testimonies from others in the course. I started to open my heart. Now I know how to make clothes. I can get a customer to make money. I got back my three kids [from relatives who were taking care of them], and they are studying. Today I feel free. I can share my story without crying."

The two widows in Peace's program at that time also had touching stories. "My husband died last February," Solange, 26 with three kids, told me. "He was sick." She had nowhere to go.

I was living a life of weeping and tears... Today I feel free, share my story without crying.

Her father had only one leg and was a beggar. When her husband died, Solange said, "It is as if the life is stopped. I lost all the hope. Also my children were transformed and became bad. But once I came here, my children were comforted. We have something to eat once a day. At the end of the program, I want a place to work, to get money, to care for my family."

Another widow, Jeannette, 37, lost her husband when he was hit by a car. She had four kids and was caring for an orphan boy, her nephew. "Life was very hard. I used to sell tomatoes, but I don't have enough to have a place, so I put tomatoes in a basket and walked around, saying 'Somebody buy?' I was always sad. But since I came here, with how people receive us, care about us, and I made friends, I started to forget my past and feel joy and hope."

Other widows received microloans (small loans) from Peace's program to sell items in the market. One was Lyduine, 41, who brought a large tablecloth she had covered with lovely hand embroidery to sell.

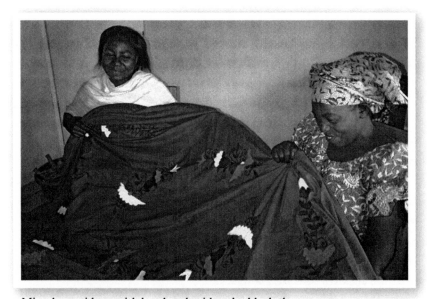

Microloan widows with hand-embroidered tablecloth

Another microloan widow, Speciose, 39, lost her husband to a sudden illness and was left with six children. "I used to sell peanuts in the street," she said, till she met "Mama Peace."

I'm doing my own business. I feel peace, I'm joyful. I do not even remember I'm a widow.

Through the loan and the small business she began, she could get food for her children and send them to school. "Now we can be persons and endure the hardness of life."

The husband of another widow with a microloan, Gloriose, age 60, had died from malaria and HIV/AIDS 16 years before. He left her with seven children ages three to thirteen. "It was very hard," she said. "My kids could no longer go to school. But now I'm doing my own business. I feel peace, I'm joyful. I do not even remember I'm a widow."

Peace tells the women they have value, they are not alone. She tells them God is going to restore their dignity. "When they come," Peace told me, "the first thing is they cry. They never think someone would care for them."

Some of the widows even end up remarrying, which is quite unusual in Africa (other than to a brother-in-law). Peace smiled when she said she has to approve the match first. After all, she is "Mama Peace" to the younger women, and she cares deeply about their future. She has even organized weddings for some of them.

Now, she added: "In the neighborhoods, they say, 'See the widow! See the widow! She had nothing to feed her children. But now see to whom God had mercy.'"

ACCOMPANYING A WIDOW

The more I learned from African widows, and others who confirmed their situation, the more concerned I became to find a way to assist these desperate women. *I have to do something*, I thought. *And if someone like me doesn't take action – after all I've seen and heard – then who will?* The idea of creating an "Adopt A Widow" program, similar to a sponsored-child program, came to mind. But somehow I needed to figure out how this would work. I'd been searching for where and how the Adopt A Widow model might apply. When I was invited to visit Peace's sewing program, I thought it might be a great fit.

The "adoption" would last for just one year in a season of support by a donor to pay for a widow's training, so she could then support herself and her family with her sewing skills. This would be like what a family member would do for a relative, especially in the African culture. The monthly costs for a donor in adopting a widow would be comparable to sponsoring a child in a developing country, a model that various organizations use successfully. Also, individuals, companies, religious groups, service clubs, extended families, and community groups could sponsor a widow.

Those I'd spoken with, from friends to African pastors, really liked the idea of Adopt A Widow. After all, many widows need both emotional and financial support. The amount that can assist a widow meaningfully in a poor country is so little compared to a western nation, and the need is so great. My Kenyan friend Dr. Emily Onyango, member of the Concerned Circle of African Women Theologians, told me she liked Adopt A Widow because it meant one could "accompany a widow along the way to independence."

I hoped that if the idea were successful, many humanitarian programs across Africa would want to start programs for widows too. When I found Peace and her program (it was the second I'd considered), it seemed a terrific match. I also had excellent recommendations about her

I'd been searching for where and how the Adopt A Widow model might apply.

from multiple sources, and I was personally impressed with her and her staff. And, she had been running the program successfully for four years.

But only two of the 22 women in Peace's program at that time were widows. One afternoon I spoke about my concern for widows with Peace and Emily Voorhies, who had introduced me to Peace. The three of us sat at an open-air restaurant on the banks of Lake Tanganyika, where hippopotamus heads would pop up occasionally among the reeds in the water. Emily was CEO of Tirzah International, a U.S.-based nonprofit benefiting women and girls around the world that had been funding Peace's program for the last four years. After all, the women were destitute and outside funding was needed.

I told Peace that if she would considering enrolling all widows in one of her two daily groups of 22 women (morning and afternoon) for her upcoming one-year course, I would find sponsors for all of them. I wanted the widows to be helped, and I wanted to show whether the model of adopting a widow could work, whether sponsors for the widows would sign up. Though I believed they would, I needed to prove it.

In the past, I said I would never do fundraising. I have friends who do that, but it wasn't my nature, or so I said. And I'd have to start by asking my personal friends to participate. But for the widows, I told Emily and Peace, I would.

Just then, Peace received a call from one of her staff and took the opportunity to ask her if she knew of any widows who would do well in the program. After a moment, Peace smiled. This person said she knew of five without even giving it much thought! It was the perfect encouragement for all three of us, at the perfect time.

It was the perfect encouragement for all three of us, at the perfect time.

Widows singing in their sewing class

As I write, 22 widows are in Peace's current program and people have signed up through Adopt A Widow to sponsor them. I recently interviewed each widow individually in Burundi and look forward to doing so again toward the end of their program. I hope to write their stories for a future book. I also hope the Adopt A Widow program will spur much help for widows across Africa, and by numerous organizations (www.adoptawidow.org).

ACTION!

What about you? How will you help Africa's widows? Throughout this book you have heard from many African voices how great the need is. What if you lived in a culture where one in four women (or more after war) is a widow? Perhaps you already do. Many of the widows are young, with small children. They have no family who can help or government that does help. How would you want others to help you if you were one of these desperate widows or one of their children?

If you are in a more developed country like my own that gives economic aid to Africa (as flawed as that can be sometimes, it still happens and can do some good), then you can write your elected

> *You can do something each year on International Widows' Day, June 23.*

officials and ask them to specify a certain amount of aid be used to help widows, with accountability mechanisms put in place. *If you live in Africa*, you can implore your elected officials to do the same, and your country's first lady to champion it, like Gabon's first lady Sylvia Bongo does.[7] You can also write to your country's representative at the United Nations, telling him or her about the huge problems of Africa's widows. You can also share with others about the need and enlist them. You can do something each year on International Widows Day, June 23. Your voice matters!

African politicians and representatives to international organizations, you have widows to represent as part of your responsibility. Please do it, and do it well. Be like President Kagame of Rwanda when he heard about widows' houses being burned down. He was outraged and had better houses rebuilt for them. As African voices have called for, legislate for land rights for women and against dehumanizing widowhood rites and forced widow inheritance, with criminal penalties. Set up human rights commissions at local levels to receive and resolve complaints. Appoint more women, and non-corruptible men and women, as judges and police to bring justice. Provide training for younger widows, scholarships for their children, and assistance for desperate older widows.

International organizations like the United Nations and African Union, be sure to include widows from conflict-ridden countries on your peacemaking and peacekeeping teams. They know war from the inside out. And often they are a high percentage of the population after war. Their voices need to be heard!

African Christian clergy and church people, you are the majority in much of Sub-Saharan Africa. Use that position well. Take courage and speak up for widows! Help care for them. Put their needs on your local and national agendas. Provide training in your churches, such as those conducted by International Justice Mission, about laws that protect women and how to write wills. Start a Justice Department in your church to accompany widows as they seek to enforce their rights. Encourage fair and wise people to run for political office and support them in any way you can. Teach Jesus' words that we are not to lord it over one another. Preach spiritual alternatives to forms of traditional African religion that unfairly blame the widow for a husband's death and call for sexual cleansing. Stand up for widows at deaths and funerals. Establish widow groups in every church and do all you can to assist them. Don't forget, you have a strong charge from your God to defend and care for widows!

Good people of every faith or no faith, remember Africa's poor widows, some of the most vulnerable people in the world, in your acts of justice and mercy!

And given the impact of Christianity in Africa, let's work together across lines of faith or no faith, regardless of other differences, to help Africa's many widows. Christian women leaders can be invited to secular strategy tables and should. International media can seek out the voices of powerful African Christian women leaders, probably all of whom will speak out strongly for widows. The media can also press leaders of African churches, which are so influential, to speak out on behalf of widows, as Bible passages support. African churches can be interviewed to state what they are doing to care for widows. Catholic and non-Catholic streams of Christianity, both so strong in Sub-Saharan Africa, can work together to help change the plight of widows.

Without such interaction between international secular, liberal, and Christian elements, and Christians working together across

dividing lines, critical mass may not be reached any time soon to turn the tide of the inhumane treatment of far too many widows. But with such interaction, I contend, we have a much better chance of seeing significant change in widows' lives.

African men, please speak up for widows! That is part of real manhood and your authentic African culture, as Ken Oketta of Uganda has shown. Can you free yourselves of a male dominance that dehumanizes not just women, but also you? All too often, this leaves you competing among yourselves and beating and oppressing women to maintain control. Be assured: this hurts not just women, but also you because you are deprived of healthy, joyful relationships. Can you engage in skills and sensitivity training and healthy peer support? Can you show you are worthy for microloans, the very small business loans being offered now across Africa, by working hard and using proceeds to support your families? Don't allow the women to have a much better reputation than you for microcredit, as they do now!

African tribal chiefs, you still have much influence in your areas, and most of you are men. What kinds of leaders will you be? Will you give respect to all in your care, including women and widows, thereby increasing your own dignity? Will you call an end to the confinement of widows, literally and figuratively, as one Nigerian chief did?

African women, you are beautiful and inspiring, please do not allow your fellow women to be mistreated as widows, or someday it could be you, your sister or mother or daughter who suffers. Elect more women to office so they will represent your interests more fully, as has happened in Rwanda.

International women, please work together for widows' sake, regardless of other differences you may have! One of the

Will you call an end to the confinement of widows, literally and figuratively?

top academic writers on women's development says women in developed nations should focus increasingly on the urgent needs and interests of women in the developing world, which includes Africa.[8] We are all sisters!

Humanitarian organizations, put widows on your agendas now! They and their children are perhaps the poorest of the poor. The most vulnerable in so many ways. Yet some of the bravest. The most noble in how they keep going. And there are so many of them. From training, to emotional healing, to gifts of mercy, especially for older widows, much needs to be done, and your actions are needed. And please, do not just lump widows in with women's programs. Widows' needs are different. They need specific programs that address their emotional and childcare issues, as well as other problems.[9]

Philanthropists, foundations, and corporations, please put widows' issues on your list of funding targets and find good people like Peace who are trustworthy and doing effective work. Please insist on programs just for widows so they are sought out in the midst of their oppression and given places to transform their lives. Fund scholarships for African women to write academically about widows and the underlying issues.

Academics, speak up! Jump on the growing bandwagon to study widows and their urgent needs and human rights violations. *Institutions*, encourage men and women to study in this huge field, and provide scholarships so more African women can document widows' and women's issues. Currently, it is estimated that only 17% of African academics are women. So women's concerns are not researched amply, much less published and shared with others.

African media, women from cities to villages need to be informed of their legal rights through radio programs that can reach many illiterate villagers. *African and international media*, tell the stories! African widows like Aunty Margaret – aided greatly by half a piece of cloth, and Eroni – the witch doctor's widow, and Kenzy – who found the broken knife on her doorstep in the DR Congo signifying her husband's death, would all make great subjects for documentaries and movies that will help spur much-needed change.

Dear widows of Africa, take heart! The head of the United Nations, Ban Ki-moon, has said you "mend the tears in social fabric."[10] You care for your children, orphans, and show courage, dignity, and resourcefulness daily by soldiering on. You are heroes, and the world is beginning to see. Gather together in associations. Elect some of your members to office. March, as African women do so well, to call attention to your human rights needs. Stand up personally to the bullies in your lives. I know it is scary but you can do it. Reach out to churches and humanitarian organizations for help. Please don't give up!

And "half-widows," those whose husbands are long missing, you are precious too. You are not forgotten. We need to understand your needs better also.

Everyone can do something! Josephine from the DR Congo, one of "Africa's Finest," wisely says if each one brings a stone, a building can be built. This is true even if you are a "poor" African woman.

Margaret Owen recounts in her book, *A World of Widows*, how a group of African women decided to help a poor widow. Her brother-in-law had seized her home for himself and kicked her out.[11] So one day, ten of the widow's friends came marching and singing to her home, carrying garden sticks and tools, ready to confront the man and kick him out. But they didn't even have to face him. Someone ran ahead to

The neglect of widows is the most significant gender human rights issue in the world today.

tell the brother-in-law. He jumped out the back window before the women even arrived and never came back. I would like to have been part of the spontaneous celebration that must have erupted from those women![12]

Owen says the neglect of widows is the most significant gender human rights issue in the world today.[13] But the issue itself is sorely neglected. That must change in order for widows to have a *whole* piece of cloth, not half at best. And it will take all of us to form a cloth that is strong, that will protect and uplift the many widows in Africa this book has addressed. No longer can we allow the millions of widows and their children to be left alone and destitute.

Those who have worked on women's land issues in Africa, including at the U.N., lament that decades of work have made some progress, but much more is needed.[14] Perhaps it takes a village, a world-sized one, for real breakthroughs to take place. Perhaps we can rise collectively as a world village that cares about some of the most oppressed women in the world, the widows of Africa, along with their children.

We too can become part of a rescue, where we grab whatever tool we have in hand – whether a voice, funds, influence, or our prayers, to come to the aid of African widows. If we do, perhaps the greedy and unjust will jump out of the back window like the brother-in-law in the story above did! Perhaps they will vacate homes they stole, so that many widows and their children can find peace and safety and be covered by a whole piece of cloth. Then we too can rejoice.

Oh, Africa, the world desperately needs to learn from the best of your culture – your care for all in your community. Please sing for widows the song we all need to hear, and that you can sing better than anyone else in the world: *Ubuntu! I am what I am because of who we all are!*

ARMY ON THE MARCH

I looked and saw a field of women. Each was sitting alone on the ground. I saw the short curly hair of one, with grey in it, and knew these were the widows of Africa, young and old alike.

Each of them cried out to God. Wailed. Alone.

These women had no one to turn to but God. The rest of the week was work, or loneliness, but this was like a sad church service, a time when the widows could allow themselves to feel again their pain and plead with God to help them. They knew he was there. Why wouldn't he help them?

Then a very large man came and stepped on the back of one of the weeping, wailing widows, pushing her down to the ground. I knew this represented the oppression of women by men in that culture. All I could do was weep at the injustice of it.

Then I heard a roar. At first I thought it was a lion coming out of the African jungle. Or was it coming from the sky? Suddenly I saw an army marching... made up of little girls and boys, crippled skinny men hobbling on crutches, muscular men carrying sick women who wanted to come too. Fire was in their eyes. Their marching steps, though not in unison like a trained army, had the same determination... They were coming forth to help the widows. They were coming in groups of one or two or three, each group to one widow. None were left out.

The sudden glow of the smiles of the widows made the day brighter.

Laughter began, then joy, a sitting down together in small groups to share a meal as food emerged from the pockets of the army. The little groups began to share stories and jokes and the luxury of a feeling of family together. But this was even richer than family by blood. It was family by choice, by sacrifice, with a sweetness and satisfaction none had known. It seemed that even the birds sang more loudly. A fresh breeze made the leaves of the *uminyinya* tree dance once again.

One widow stood and in her old dress of a once-beautiful African fabric began a dance of joy. There was no music save what was in her heart, but all seemed to hear it. The army of family could see what she had looked like when she was younger, without the burden of widowhood strapped tightly on her back. She was so beautiful.

People all over began to clap and rise to their feet. They thought they heard music, but did not know where it was coming from. Their joy was so great their minds let go, and their hearts grew big. They entered into the stream of gladness with abandon, their bodies reaching out in dance to life.

They became a teaming mass, undulating in the breeze and their joy that enveloped them. All of the people began to feel they had never known such happiness. No one was alone.

NOTES

CHAPTER 1 – WOMEN AS 'PROPERTY'

1 Okoye, Pat U., *Widowhood: A Natural or Cultural Tragedy*, Enugu: Nucik Publishers, 1995, 184.
2 Mombo is currently the Deputy Vice Chancellor of St. Paul's University in Kenya. It is estimated that about 17% of academic leadership positions in Sub-Saharan Africa are held by women. Mombo, Esther, "Transforming Our World of Faith: Attitudes About Sexual Harassment and Abuse." Speech given at "Equal to Serve: Gender and Authentic Biblical Leadership" Conference, Limuru, Kenya, July 20-22, 2012.
3 Though some experts contend that colonialism worsened male patriarchy by enshrining male domination in western-style laws. See Malukeke, M.J., "Culture, Tradition, Custom, Law and Gender Equality," Presentation delivered at the Conference of the South African Chapter of the International Association of Women Judges, 12-13 August 2011, Potchefstroom, South Africa. PER, 2012 Volume 15 No 1, 15/428.
4 Mombo, Esther, *op cit.*
5 Email from Emily Onyango to the author, 27 January 2014.
6 Statistics-Africa, Focus, International, http://www.focusintl.com/statr1a1.htm, accessed 5/14/2008.
7 Kimani, Lillian, "Gender Justice as the Center of the Christian Faith," Speech given at "Equal to Serve" Conference, Limuru, Kenya, 2012.
8 Wasonga, Jenipha, "Wading the Waters of Marriage." Speech given at "Equal to Serve" Conference, Limuru, Kenya, 2012.
9 Okoye, Ifeoma, *The Trial and Other Stories*, New York/Lagos/London: African Heritage Press, 2005, 2.
10 Akujobi, Remi, "Yesterday You Were Divorced, Today I am a Widow: An Appraisal of Widowhood Practices and the Effects on the Psyche of Widows in Africa," Department of English and Literary Studies, 13.
11 Okoye, Pat, *op cit,* 127.
12 Dennis, Suzanna and Zuckerman, Elaine (2006). "Gender Guide to World Bank and IMF Policy-Based Lending," Gender Action, December, 9. http://www.oxfam.org.uk/resources/policy/debt_aid/bn_wbimf_blindspot.html, Accessed 28 October 2007.
13 Owen, Margaret, *A World of Widows*, London and New Jersey: Zed Books Ltd, 1996, 51.
14 Limann, Leda Hasila, "Widowhood Rites and the Rights of Women

in Africa: The Ugandan Experience," Submitted in partial fulfillment of the requirements for the LLM Degree in Human Rights and Democratisation in Africa, Faculty of Law, Makerere University, Kampala, Uganda, October 2003, 47.

15 Human Rights Watch, "Discrimination in Property and Inheritance Rights and HIV/AIDS," http://www.hrw.org/reports/2003/africa1203/5.htm, accessed 11/9/2012.

16 Okoye, Pat U., *Widowhood: A Natural or Cultural Tragedy,* Enugu: Nucik Publishers, 1995, 231.

17 Kodia, *op cit.*

18 Odimmegwa, Augustine Okwunna, "Widowhood and the Dignity of Womanhood in Igboland: A Pastoral Challenge to the Discipleship of the Roman Catholic Church in Igboland," Ph.D. Dissertation, Fordham University, New York, 2010, 53.

19 Kodia, David, "Balancing a Gendered Worldview: Politics and Religion in Focus," Speech given at "Equal to Serve" Conference, Limuru, Kenya, 2012.

20 Asiimwe, Florence Akiiki and Crankshaw, Owen, "The Impact of Customary Laws on Inheritance: A Case Study of Widows in Urban Uganda," *Journal of Law and Conflict Resolution,* Vol. 3(1), pp. 7-13, January 2011, 7, 9.

21 IRIN PlusNews, "Kenya: Protecting Widows from Dangerous Customs," http://www.plusnews.org/PrintReport. aspx?ReportId=72821, accessed 5/2/2008, 1.

22 As cited in International Justice Mission, Casework Bulletin, 13 April 2010, http://www.ijm.org/articles/caseworkbulletin, accessed 7/5/2010.

23 Peterman, Amber. 'Widowhood and Asset Inheritance in Sub-Saharan Africa: Empirical Evidence from Fifteen Countries.' *Development Policy Review.* Vol. 30, 2012, 543-57.

24 Immigration and Refugee Board of Canada, "Ashanti widow rituals, steps required, whether the widow can refuse to participate, whether she would be required to marry her husband's relative, and consequences for refusal [GHA38600.E], 07 May 2002, http://www. ecoi.net/local_link/176988/293909_de.html.

25 United Nations, "International Widows Day, Background Information, http://www.un.org/en/events/widowsday/background. shtml, 1. "Widows, Aids, Health and Human Rights in Africa, Vanessa von Struensee, JD, MPH, 2004.

26 Immigration and Refugee Board of Canada (2002) 'Ashanti widow rituals, steps required, whether the widow can refuse to participate, whether she would be required to marry her husband's relative, and consequences for refusal' [GHA38600.E]. 07 May, http://www.ecoi. net/local_link/176988/293909_de.html.

NOTES

United Nations, "International Widows Day," *op cit.* Also see
United Nations, Division for the Advancement of Women (2001).
'Widowhood: invisible women, secluded or excluded,' *Women2000,*
December, 7.

27 Widows Rights International, "2012 International Widow's Day: Will
the widow's plight be over?" No. 20, August 2012.

28 United Nations, "International Widows Day, Background
Information, http://www.un.org/en/events/widowsday/background.
shtml, 2.

29 Von Struensee, Vanessa, JD, MPH, "Widows, Aids, Health and
Human Rights in Africa, 2004, 21 and Modern Ghana News,
"Widowhood Rites Still Rife in Northern Regions," September 30,
2010. http://ww.modernghana.com/news/298544/1/widowhood-rites-
still-rife-in-northern-regions.html.

30 Okoye, Pat U., *Widowhood: A Natural or Cultural Tragedy,* Enugu:
Nucik Publishers, 1995.

31 Okoye, *op cit,* 46.

32 Okoye, *op cit,* 85.

33 Okoye, *op cit,* 41-126.

34 Odimmegwa, Augustine Okwunna, *op cit,* 172.

35 Kabonde, Mulambya P. (1996) 'Widowhood in Zambia: The Effects
of Ritual,' in *Groaning in Faith: African Women in the Household
of God,* Kanyoro, Musimbi R.A. and Njoroge, Nyambura J., eds.,
Nairobi: Acton Publishers, 198.

36 Okoye explains that it is a popular belief among pagans that the
spirit of a dead husband will relentlessly haunt any of his relations
who take over the widow wife unless the deceased is accorded full
funeral rites. Through these rites, the widow supposedly rectifies
a breach of conduct or prevents its occurrence. Okoye calls this
enforcement by the community due to traditional beliefs a kind
of "cosmic dragnet" that calls for immediate punishment. It is
considered an "abomination," she says, a "sacrilege," if a woman
contributes to the rejection of her dead husband into the bosom of
his forebears. "Anything that deprives him of this privilege deserves
any amount of venom unleashed against it, in the way of retaliation
and vengeance." If the dead husband is deprived of the rites, it is
believed that epidemics, diseases, famine, pestilence, and even deaths
of extended family members may result. So "the whole community
rises in arms against the offender." "The whole army of extended
family members march on any woman who contravenes traditional
widowhood practices." Okoye, *op cit,* 131, 132, 222.

37 Human Rights Watch, Discrimination in Property and Inheritance
Rights and HIV/AIDS, 2003, http://wwwhrw.org/reports/2003/
africa1203/5.htm, 1.

38 Odimmegwa, Augustine Okwunna, *op cit,* 21.

39 Okoye, *op cit.*

40 Odimmegwa, Augustine Okwunna, *op cit,* 14.

41 Oche, Michael, Nigeria: Life After Our Husbands' Death is Terrible, Widows Cry Out," *AllAfrica,* 24 June 2012, http://allafrica.com/stories/printable/201206250277.html, accessed 9/5/2012.

42 (1) Shisanya, Constance R.A. (1996). 'Death Rituals: The Case of the Abaluhya of Western Kenya,' in *Groaning in Faith: African Women in the Household of God,* Kanyoro, Musimbi R.A. and Njoroge, Nyambura, eds. Nairobi: Acton Publishers, 187, 193. (2) Kabonde, Mulambya P. (1996) 'Widowhood in Zambia: The Effects of Ritual,' in *Groaning in Faith: African Women in the Household of God, op cit,* 198. (3) Nwachuku, Daisy N. (1992) 'The Christian Widow in African Culture' in Oduyoye, Mercy Amba & Kanyoro, Musimbi R.A., eds. (1992) *The Will to Arise: Women, Tradition, and the Church in Africa.* Eugene: Wipf & Stock Publishers, 63.

43 Okoye, *op cit,* 141.

44 Limann, Leda Hasila, *op cit,* 59.

45 Limann, Leda Hasila, *op cit,* 30.

46 Nwachuku, Daisy N. (1992) 'The Christian Widow in African Culture' in Oduyoye, Mercy Amba & Kanyoro, Musimbi R.A., eds. (1992) *The Will to Arise: Women, Tradition, and the Church in Africa.* Eugene: Wipf & Stock Publishers, 72.

47 Okoye, *op cit,* 13.

48 Odimmegwa, *op cit,* 36.

49 Limann, Leda Hasila, *op cit,*1, 2.

50 Agot, Kawango, et al (2010). 'Widow Inheritance and HIV Prevalence in Bondo District, Kenya: Baseline Results form a Prospective Cohort Study,' PLoS ONE, Vol 5, Issue 11, 1-5.

51 George, Tayo O., "Policy Response to Widowhood Rites among the Awori of Ogun State, Nigeria," *American International Journal of Contemporary Research,* Vol. 2, No. 5, May 2012, 188.

52 Asiimwe, Florence Akiiki and Crankshaw, Owen, "The Impact of Customary Laws on Inheritance: A Case Study of Widows in Urban Uganda," *Journal of Law and Conflict Resolution,* Vol. 3(1), pp. 7-13, January 2011, 7.

53 Oche, Michael, Nigeria: Life After Our Husbands' Death is Terrible, Widows Cry Out," *AllAfrica,* 24 June 2012, http://allafrica.com/stories/printable/201206250277.html, accessed 9/5/2012.

54 United Nations, Division for the Advancement of Women (2001). 'Widowhood: invisible women, secluded or excluded,' *Women2000,* December, 11.

55 Widows Rights International (2012) '2012 International Widow's Day: Will the widow's plight be over?' No. 20, August.

56 107th Congress, 2D Session, H. Con. Res. 421, "Recognizing the importance of inheritance rights of women in Africa," June 18, 2002.

57 *New African Magazine* (2012). 'Empowering Widows through Education,' May, 49.

58 Widows Rights International, "Women's Inheritance Rights to Land and Housing," Women's Land Link Africa, http://www.widowsrights.org/landlink.html, accessed 5/2/08, 1.

59 Uniformly, those who write about widows in Africa agree that there is a dearth of statistics about them. So, until more research is done, we can only extrapolate figures from what we do know currently to estimate how many widows in Africa are suffering. If, at this writing, Sub-Saharan Africa has a population of approximately 874 million (The World Bank, Sub-Saharan Africa, http://data.worldbank.org/region/sub-saharan-africa. Figures for 2011), and if an estimated 50% are females, that means approximately 437 million females. If an estimated 58% of those females are 15 and over (The World Bank, reference just cited), that means approximately 253 million females 15 and over. If an estimated one in four of these women are widows ("Women's Inheritance Rights to Land and Housing," Widows Rights International, endnote 58.), that means a staggering 63 million widows in Sub-Saharan Africa. Further, an estimated 30% of Sub-Saharan Africa's population is hungry ("Sub-Saharan Africa Hunger and Poverty Facts," World Hunger, http://www.worldhunger.org/articles/Learn/africa_hunger_facts.html. Figures for 2011). I can only conclude that a good portion of these are widows, who are called the poorest of Africa's poor. A 2010 study (Dutt, Vijay, *Invisible Forgotten Sufferers, The Plight of Widows Around the World, Why the UN Should Recognize International Widows Day, A Research Study commissioned by the Loomba Foundation and presented to the United Nations on International Widows Day, 23 June 2010, Research by Risto F. Harma,*New Delhi: Konark Publishers Pvt Ltd, 2010, 1-5, 131) estimated there are 245 million widows in the world (though two international widowhood organizations consider this figure to be low), and approximately half of these widows live in significant poverty. Therefore, I would estimate that at least half of what I estimate to be 63 million widows in Sub-Saharan Africa, or approximately 31 million widows, are desperately poor. Adding in their children, especially for the many young widows, creates a much larger number. Wives of the missing, especially in conflict areas, could swell the numbers of widows more.

60 George, Tayo, *op cit,* 187.

61 Odimmegwa, *op cit,* 164.

62 Limann, Leda Hasila, *op cit,*97.

63 Pew Forum on Religion and Public Life, 'Tolerance and Tension:

Islam and Christianity in Sub-Saharan Africa.' Poll, April
2010. http://www.pewforum.org/executive-summary-islam-and-
christianity-in-sub-saharan-africa.aspx. Accessed 23/4/2013.
64 *Ibid.*

CHAPTER 2 – UNDER RWANDA'S SPREADING UMINYINYA TREE

1 Survivors Fund, Supporting Survivors of the Rwanda Genocide,
   http://survivors-fund.org.uk/resources/rwandan-history/statistics/.
   Accessed 3 August 2013.
2 *Ibid.* A recent report puts the number at 1,952,078.
3 Stephen Kinzer tells this story of Kagame in *A Thousand Hills:
   Rwanda's Rebirth and the Man Who Dreamed It*, New York City:
   Wiley, 2008.
4 *Ibid.*
5 Youth With A Mission Rwanda works with more than 700 widows in
   four areas around the capital of Rwanda, among its various activities.
   www.ywamrwanda.com. It is affiliated with Youth With A Mission,
   which at this writing has more than 1,100 locations in 180 countries
   around the world. www.ywam.org.
6 She was referring to the biblical passages of Isaiah 54:4-5 and Psalms
   68:5.
7 AVEGA Agahozo, http://survivors-fund.org.uk/what-we-do/local-
   partners/avega/, accessed 1 September 2013.
8 International Justice Mission has, at this writing, justice professionals
   who work in their communities in 16 field offices in Asia, Africa
   and Latin America. Their work is to secure tangible and sustainable
   protection of national laws through local court systems. www.ijm.org.

CHAPTER 3 – THREADS OF HOPE IN GHANA

1 "Profile of the Ghana Land Administration Project," Suleiman
   Mustapha, *The Statesman*, 26/07/2006,
   http://www.thestatesmanonline.com/pages/news_detail.
   php?section=9&newsid=91, accessed 12/7/2007.
2 "Language and Religion," Ghana Embassy, http://www.
   ghanaembassy.org/index.php?page=language-and-religion, accessed
   26 July 2013.
3 "Ghana's extravagant funerals drive families into debt," Lily Mensah,
   World News, 12 June 2013, http://www.upi.com/Top_News/World-
   News/2013/06/12/Ghanas-extravagant-funerals-drive-families-into-
   debt/PC-9771371075364/. Accessed 13 September 2013.
4 A school principal told me about this newspaper story, which I have

not been able to locate. Her name is not used because of her request for anonymity.

5 FIDA is an acronym for the name of the group in French. In English it's the International Federation of Women Lawyers.

CHAPTER 4 – VALOR IN UGANDA

1 "Health and mortality survey among internally displaced persons in Gulu, Kitgum and Pader Districts, Northern Uganda," The Republic of Uganda Ministry of Health, July 2005. http://www.who.int/hac/crises/uga/sitreps/Ugandamortsurvey.pdf, accessed 3 August 2013.
2 *Ibid.*
3 Dixon, Robin, 'Uganda widow wins compensation after fight,' *Los Angeles Times,* 29 April 2013.
4 IFAD, International Fund for Agricultural Development, United Nations, "Uganda, Ghana and Cote d'Ivoire – The Situation of Widows," http://www.ifad.org/gender/learning/challenges/widows/55.htm, accessed 3 August 2013.
5 Uganda Bureau of Statistics, Uganda National Household Survey Findings 2009/2010, http://www.ubos.org/UNHS9010/chapter 11_widows.html, accessed 3 August 2013.
6 Bulletin of the World Health Organization, Koenig, M.A. et al, 'Domestic violence in rural Uganda: evidence from a community-based study, 2003. 81 (1).
7 This booklet and its development are described in more detail in the last chapter.
8 "Principles and Practices of Customary Tenure in Acholiland." For more information write to Ken Oketta, Ker Kwaro Acholi, PO Box 54, Gulu, Uganda.

CHAPTER 5 – HONOR IN A SOUTH AFRICAN TOWNSHIP

1 "South Africa's Unemployment Rate Increases to 23.5% (Update 2)," Seria, N. and Cohen, M., May 5, 2009, http://www.bloomberg.com/apps/news?pid=newsarchive&sid=aoB7RbcZCRfU, accessed 9 August 2013.
2 "World: Africa, South Africa's Rape Shock," 19 January 1999. http://news.bbc.co.uk/2/hi/africa/258446.stm, accessed 9 August 2013.
3 "South African Rape Survey Shock," 18 June 2009, http://news.bbc.co.uk/2/hi/africa/8107039.stm, accessed 9 August 2013.
4 "South Africa Profile," BBC News, 9 May 2013, http://www.bbc.co.uk/news/world-africa-14094760, accessed 9 August 2013.
5 "Sixth Time's the charm: Polygamist South African president Jacob Zuma beams with delight as he marries Gloria Ngema (while his

other three wives look on), Maclean, S., *Mail Online,* 21 April 2012, http://www.dailymail.co.uk/news/article-2133220/Polygamist-South-African-president-Jacob-Zuma-marries-Gloria-Ngema-wives-look-on.html, accessed 9 August 2013.
Zuma was married twice before his four current wives. According to the referenced report, he divorced one wife and the next year another wife committed suicide.

6 "Women's Month, A Centenary of working together towards a sustainable women empowerment and gender equality," South African Government Information, http://www.info.gov.za/speech/DynamicAction?pageid=461&sid=33076&tid=93679, accessed 9 August 2013.

7 See "South Africa: National Widows Forum Launched in Polokwane," South African Government (Pretoria), 26 July 2013, http://allafrica.com/stories/201307270110.html, accessed 9 August 2013.

CHAPTER 6 – RICHES IN THE CONGO

1 Hochschild, Adam, *King Leopold's Ghost: A Story of Greed, Terror and Heroism in Colonial Africa,* Boston: Houghton Mifflin, 1999.

2 For an excellent book about his life, see *In His Footsteps: Living on the Brink of Disaster in the Congo,* Wrong, Michaela, Harrisburg: Fourth Estate, 2001.

3 An acclaimed book about this war is *Africa's World War: Congo, the Rwandan Genocide, and the Making of a Continental Catastrophe,* Pruner, Gérard, Oxford: Oxford University Press, 2011.

4 Pruner, Gérard, *Africa's World War: Congo, the Rwandan Genocide, and the Making of a Continental Catastrophe,* Oxford: Oxford University Press, 2011.

5 "Conflict Minerals in Your Mobile — Why Congo's War Matters," Jegarajah, Sri, 26 November 2012, http://www.cnbc.com/id/49961559, accessed 11 August 2013.

6 Hope International is a microloan agency that works in Africa, Asia, Eastern Europe, and Latin America. www.hopeinternational.org.

CHAPTER 7 – BREAKTHROUGH IN ZAMBIA

1 Deuteronomy 27:19, New International Version.

2 Zambia – Religions, Encyclopedia of the Nations, http://www.nationsencyclopedia.com/Africa/Zambia-RELIGIONS.html, accessed 3 August 2013.

3 *Ibid.*

4 Zambia, The World Fact Book, 2009, https://www.cia.gov/

library/publications/the-world-factbook/rankorder/2155rank.
html?countryName=Lesotho&countryCode=LT&regionCode
=af#LT, accessed 17 August 2013.

5 Namutowe, Judith, "Zambia: Standing up to malnutrition," 30 July
2013, http://allafrica.com/stories/201307301245.html, accessed 19
August 2013.

6 President's Malaria Initiative, Zambia, April 2013, http://www.
fightingmalaria.gov/countries/profiles/zambia_profile.pdf, accessed
19 August 2013.

7 "Toothless law under review to curb rising cases of property
grabbing, Lusaka Times, 21 May 2011, http://www.lusakatimes.
com/2011/05/21/toothless-law-review-curb-rising-cases-property-
grabbing/, accessed 19 August 2013.

8 The documentary is "Pray the Devil Back to Hell." The woman who
led the movement, Leymah Gbowee, eventually won the Nobel
Peace Prize for her efforts.

9 Deuteronomy 27:19, New International Version.

10 Isaiah 10:1-2, New International Version.

11 James 1:27, New International Version.

CHAPTER 8 – TWO OF AFRICA'S FINEST

1 Pew Forum on Religion and Public Life, 'Tolerance and Tension:
Islam and Christianity in Sub-Saharan Africa.' Poll, April 2010.
http://features.pewforum.org/africa/country.php?c=51, accessed 10
August 2013.

CHAPTER 9 – RELIGION: HELPING OR HURTING?

1 Odimmegwa, Augustine Okwunna, "Widowhood and the Dignity of
Womanhood in Igboland: A Pastoral Challenge to the Discipleship
of the Roman Catholic Church in Igboland," Ph.D. Dissertation,
Graduate School of Religion and Religious Education, Fordham
University, New York, 2010, 3, 196.

2 "Notoriously religious": Mombo, Esther, "Christian Response to
Gender Issues in Africa in the Era of HIV and AIDS." Speech given
at "Equal to Serve: Gender and Authentic Biblical Leadership"
Conference, Limuru, Kenya, July 20-22, 2012. Dr. Mombo is the
Academic Dean at St. Paul's University in Kenya.
Culture and religion embrace all areas of life: Kanyoro, Musimbi,
"Engineered Communal Theology: African Women's Contribution
to Theology in the Twenty-First Century," *Feminist Theology*, May
2001, Vol 9 No 27, 36. http://fth.sagepub.com/content/9/27/36.extract.
Accessed 8/15/2012. Ms. Musimbi is a Nobel Peace Prize Nominee.

3   The Pew Forum Religion and Public Life conducted a study of
    25,000 African in 19 countries in 2010. The findings are given in
    'Tolerance and Tension: Islam and Christianity in Sub-Saharan
    Africa.' Poll, April 2010. http://www.pewforum.org/executive-
    summary-islam-and-christianity-in-sub-saharan-africa.aspx.
    Accessed 23/4/2013.
4   *Ibid.* The only country not included is Burundi, which was not
    included in the survey, however, its culture is very similar to Rwanda,
    which was included, given that they were both in the same country
    prior to colonialization and have the same two main tribes.
5   *Ibid.*
6   *Ibid.*
7   *Ibid.*
8   *Ibid.*
9   United Nations, Division for the Advancement of Women (2001).
    'Widowhood: invisible women, secluded or excluded,' *Women2000*,
    December, 11.
10 Wanyeki, L. Muthoni, ed., *Women and Land in Africa, Culture,
    Religion and Realizing Women's Rights*, South Africa: David Philip
    Publishers, London/New York: Zed Books, 2003, 27.
11 Crane, Jane L., "Map for Gender Reconciliation," in "Empowering
    Women and Men to Use their Gifts Together in Advancing the
    Gospel," Alvera Mickelson, ed., Lausanne Occasional Paper No. 53,
    Lausanne Committee for World Evangelization, in *A New Vision,
    A New Heart, A Renewed Call*, David Claydon, ed., Volume Two,
    Pasadena, CA: William Carey Library, 2005. The Map in entirety can
    be ordered from www.equalitydepot.com.
12 Description of the Cape Town 2010 Third World Congress by
    Christianity Today, Online Report from Cape Town, South Africa, 20
    October 2010.
13 Mombo, Esther, *op cit.*
14 Odimmegwa, *op cit*, 72.
15 Onuh, Emmanuel, "Widows in the Church: Any Protection and
    Help?" in *Widowhood in the Church and Society*, ed. Aloysius C.
    Obiwulu (Enugu, Nigeria: Delta Publications Nigeria Ltd., 2009), 94,
    as reported in Odimmegwa, *op cit,* 107.
16 Odimmegwa, *op cit*, 174.
17 Odimmegwa, *op cit*, 155-7.
18 Odimmegwa, *op cit*, 157-8.
19 Odimmegwa, *op cit*, 160.
20 Mbugua, Judy, ed., *Our Time Has Come, African Christian Women
    Address the Issues of Today*, Grand Rapids: Baker Book House, 1994,
    79.
21 Okoye, Pat U., *Widowhood: A Natural or Cultural Tragedy*, Nucik

Publishers, Enugu, Nigeria, 1995, 154.
22 Deuteronomy 27:19, New International Version.
23 Isaiah 10:1-2, New International Version.
24 Job 22: 9-10, New International Version.
25 Deuteronomy 10:17-18, New International Version.
26 Proverbs 15:25, New International Version.
27 Malachi 3:5, New International Version.
28 James 1:27, New International Version.
29 Isaiah 1:17, New International Version.
30 Deuteronomy 26:12, New International Version.
31 Deuteronomy 14:29, New International Version.
32 For more passages about widows: see Jeremiah 22:3, Psalms 68:4-5,
   Exodus 22:22-23, Malachi 3:5, Psalms 146:9, Isaiah 54:4-5,
   1 Timothy 5:5.
   Grabbing land/goods: Micah 2:9, Proverbs 23:10-11,
   Proverbs 22:22-23.
   Helping the poor and justice: one example of many is
   Proverbs 31:8-9.
33 Skype interview with the author, July 2011.
34 Okoye, Pat, *op cit*, 13.
35 *Op cit*, 222.
36 *Op cit,* 131-2.
37 Okoye, Pat, *op cit*, 45.
38 *Op cit*, 141.
39 Okoye, Pat, *op cit*, 135.
40 Odimmegwa, op cit, 188.
41 Kodia, David, "Gendered Economics and Social Privileges," Speech
   given at "Equal to Serve: Gender and Authentic Biblical Leadership"
   Conference, Limuru, Kenya, July 20-22, 2012.
42 An excellent book to study the debate is Cunningham, Loren, and
   Hamilton, David, with Janice Rogers (2000). *Why Not Women:
   A Fresh Look at Scripture on Women in Missions, Ministry, and
   Leadership.* Seattle: YWAM Publishing.
43 1 Corinthians 11:3. The Greek word for "head" is *kephale*.
44 Verses 11 and 12.
45 Matthew 20:25, Mark 10:42, Luke 22:25.
46 1 Timothy 2:12.
47 The Greek word used here is *authentein*.
48 One is theologian Linda Belleville in "Teaching and Usurping
   Authority: 1 Timothy 2:11-15" in *Discovering Biblical Equality*, Eds.,
   Pierce, R.W. and Groothuis, R.M, Downer's Grove: InterVarsity
   Press, 2005.
49 I Timothy 3:1-12. Titus 1:6-9.
50 This is the Greek word *diakonos*. Romans 16:1.

51 Romans 16:7.
52 "The Homilies of John Chrysostom, Nicene and Post-Nicene Fathers," Series 1, 11:555. Eerdmans. 1956.
53 Ephesians 5:22.
54 Ephesians 5:25.
55 1 Peter 3:7.
56 John 13.34, Romans 12:10, Galatians 5:13.
57 Mombo, Esther, "Transforming Our World of Faith: Attitudes About Sexual Harassment and Abuse." Speech given at "Equal to Serve: Gender and Authentic Biblical Leadership" Conference, Limuru, Kenya, July 20-22, 2012.
58 *The Cape Town Commitment: A Confession of Faith and a Call to Action.* The Lausanne Movement (Great Britain: 2011), II E 3C.
59 Philip Payne teaches on 12 passages of Scripture that affirm mutuality in marriage. Payne, Phillip, "Examining the Twelve Pillars of Male Hierarchy," presented in Limuru, Kenya, at the Equal to Serve Conference and "A New Creation, A New Tradition," conference presentation in Houston, Texas, on April 27-28, 2012. DVD available from www.cbeinternational.org.
60 "Apostolic Letter *Mulieris Dignitatatem* of the Supreme Pontiff John Paul II on the Dignity and Vocation of Women on the Occasion of the Marian Year," John Paul II, 15 August 1988, Apostolic Letter, 11, http://www.vatican.va/holy_father/john_paul_ii/apost_letters/documents/hf_jp-ii_apl_1508..., accessed 3/25/2008.
61 Genesis 2:18. In the original Hebrew of the Old Testament, the phrase used to describe woman is *ēzer kĕnegdÔ*.
62 Kaiser, Walter C. (2011). "Correcting Caricatures: The Biblical Teaching on Women," http://www.walterckaiserjr.com/women.html. Also see http://www.walterckaiserjr.com/womenpage2.html, . Accessed 10 December 2011.
63 Kaiser, Walter C., http://www.walterckaiserjr.com/women.html, 3.
64 Genesis 1:26-28.
65 Nicole, Roger. 1984. "Biblical Concept of Women," *Evangelical Dictionary of Theology*. Grand Rapids: Baker Book House. Also see Kaiser, Walter C., op cit, 1-2.
66 These two works are: *Bado Tuko Sambamba*, George, Janet, *Side by Side, A Concise Explanation of Biblical Equality,"* Minneapolis: Christians for Biblical Equality, 2009, Translated by Philip Owasi, and Berkeley, A. and *Masomo Juu ya Usawa wa KiBiblia*, Mickelson, Alvera, *Studies on Biblical Equality, 12 Lesson Outlines for Personal or Group Studies*, Minneapolis: Christians for Biblical Equality, Translated by Philip Owasi.
67 Cunningham, Loren, and Hamilton, David, with Janice Rogers (2000). *Why Not Women: A Fresh Look at Scripture on Women in*

Missions, Ministry, and Leadership. Seattle: YWAM Publishing.

68 For an excellent study on how the Greeks influenced the Rome-conquered Jews away from the dignity women had in the Old Testament, as well as a very readable study of the controversial Scripture passages about women, I highly recommend Cunningham, Loren, and Hamilton, David, with Janice Rogers (2000). *Why Not Women: A Fresh Look at Scripture on Women in Missions, Ministry, and Leadership*. Seattle: YWAM Publishing.

69 Mark 16:14, Luke 10:39-42.

70 John 4:4-42.

71 Matthew 9:9-10, John 20:14-18 and Mark 16:14.

72 Luke 11:27-28.

73 Mark 15:40-41, Luke 8:1-3.

74 Acts 1:14-15.

75 Acts 2:4.

76 Acts 2:16-18.

77 For Paul, see Romans 16:3 and 2 Timothy 4:19, 1 Corinthians 11:5, 1 Corinthians 1:11 and Colossians 4:15, Philippians 4:2-3 and Romans 16:1-15, 2 Timothy 2:2 and Ephesians 4:7-8, 11, and Romans 16:7. Also see Acts 21:9, Acts 18:18, 19, 26, and 2 John 1, 10.

78 Luke 2:36-38.

79 John 19:25-27.

80 Luke 7:12-17.

81 Luke 18:1-8.

82 Mark 12:38-44, Luke 20:45-47, Luke 21:1-4.

83 1 Timothy 5:3-16.

84 1 Timothy 5:3-16.

85 Matthew 19:3-8.

86 Odimmegwa, *op cit*, 3, 195-6.

87 Odimmegwa, *op cit*, 37, 51, 72, 175-7, 189-90, 192-6.

88 Adamu, Fatima L. and Para-Mallam, Oluwafunmilayo J. (2012). 'The role of religion in women's campaigns for legal reform in Nigeria.' *Development in Practice*. August, Vol. 22 Issue 5/6, 803-818.

89 http://www.saddleback.com, accessed 2/12/2013.

90 "Widowhood: invisible women, secluded or excluded," *Women 2000*, Division for the Advancement of Women, United Nations, December 2001.

CHAPTER 10 – A WHOLE PIECE OF CLOTH

1 These include Oxfam, Landesa, Human Rights Watch, and various arms of the United Nations.

2 I highly recommend the following:
Ba, Mariama, *So Long A Letter*. Senegal: Nouvelles Editions

Africaines du Senegal, Long Grove: Waveland Press, Inc., 1980. Considered one of the top 100 African books of the 20th century and translated into 16 languages. A superb semi-autobiographical account by a brilliant Muslim woman school teacher in Senegal who herself was widowed.

Sinyangwe, B., *A Cowrie of Hope.* Oxford: Heinemann Educational Publishers, 2000. The author, a widower, tells the story of a poor and illiterate African widow. It has amazing characters and an uplifting, surprising, and sometimes humorous story.

Okoye, Ifeoma, *The Trial and Other Stories*, Lagos: African Heritage Press, 2005. A collection of clever short stories about widows. The title story is about a young widow who has to face the *umuada*, her husband's female relatives, and prove her innocence in his death.

3 http://www.un.org/en/events/widowsday/.

4 Dutt, Vijay, *Invisible Forgotten Sufferers, The Plight of Widows Around the World, Why the UN Should Recognize International Widows Day, A Research Study commissioned by the Loomba Foundation and presented to the United Nations on International Widows Day, 23 June 2010, Research by Risto F. Harma,* New Delhi: Konark Publishers Pvt Ltd, 2010, 1-5.

5 Owen, Margaret, *A World of Widows*, London and New Jersey: Zed Books Ltd, 1996, vii. Currently Owen is director of Widows for Peace through Democracy. www.widowsforpeace.org. Hovington, Kathryn, "On the Run with Margaret Owen OBE," The International Criminal Law Bureau Blog, May 9, 2012.

6 "Burundi Profile," BBC News Africa, 5 Feb 2014. http://www.bbc.co.uk/news/world-africa-13085064, accessed 13 Feb 2014.

7 *New African* (2011). 'Many First Ladies do Excellent Work,' Issue 508, 20-22, July.

8 Nussbaum, Martha (2000). *Women and Human Development: The Capabilities Approach.* New York: Cambridge University Press, 7.

9 IFAD, the International Fund for Agricultural Development, part of the United Nations, agrees that widows and their dependent children are an important sub-group of women in terms of targeting for specific programs. "Uganda, Ghana and Cote d'Ivoire – The Situation of Widows,' http://www.ifad.org/gender/learning/challenges/widows/55.htm, accessed 8 September 2013.

10 Ban Ki-moon (2011). Secretary General's Message for 2011, International Widow' Day, June 23. http://www.un.org/en/events/widowsday/2011/sgmessage.shtml, accessed 15 September 2013.

11 Owen, Margaret, *A World of Widows*, London and New Jersey: Zed Books Ltd, 1996, 189-190.

12 Owen, Margaret, *A World of Widows*, London and New Jersey: Zed Books Ltd, 1996, 189-190.

13 Widows for Peace through Democracy, Speech by Margaret Owen, http://www.widowsforpeace.org/, accessed 29 September 2013.
14 Kimani, Mary (2008). "Women Struggle to Secure Land Rights: Hard Fight for Access and Decision Making Power," *Africa Renewal,* United Nations Department of Public Information, Vol. 22, No. 1, April.

BIBLIOGRAPHY

Adamu, F.L. and Para-Mallam, O. J. (2012). 'The role of religion in women's campaigns for legal reform in Nigeria.' *Development in Practice*. August, Vol. 22 Issue 5/6, 803-818.

Adetunji, J.A. (2002) 'HIV/AIDS and young age widowhood in Sub-Saharan Africa.' *Journal of Health and Human Services Administration*. Winter 2001/Spring 2002, Vol 24, Issue3/4, 259-278.

Agot, Kawango, et al (2010). 'Widow Inheritance and HIV Prevalence in Bondo District, Kenya: Baseline Results form a Prospective Cohort Study,' PLoS ONE, Vol 5, Issue 11, 1-5.

Akujobi, R. (2009) 'Yesterday You Were Divorced, Today I am a Widow: An Appraisal of Widowhood Practices and the Effects on the Psyche of Widows in Africa.' December.

Asiimwe, F.A. & Crankshaw, O. (2011) 'The Impact of Customary Laws on Inheritance: A Case Study of Widows in Urban Uganda.' *Journal of Law and Conflict Resolution*, Vol 3(1), pp. 7-13, Jan.

Auikukwei, R.M. & Ngare, D. & Sidle, J.E. & Ayuku, D.O. & Baliddawa, J. & Greene, J.Y. (2007) 'Social and cultural significance of the sexual cleansing ritual and its impact on HIV prevention strategies in Western Kenya.' *Sexuality and Culture*. Summer, Vol 11, Issue 3, 32-50.

AVEGA Agahozo, http://survivors-fund.org.uk/what-we-do/local-partners/avega/, accessed 1 September 2013.

Ba, M. (1980) *So Long A Letter*. Senegal: Nouvelles Editions Africaines du Senegal, Long Grove: Waveland Press, Inc.

Cattell, M.G. (2003) 'African Widows: Anthropological and Historical Perspectives.' *Journal of Women and Aging*. Vol 15, Issue 2/3, 49.

Congress of the U.S., 107th Congress (2002) 2D Session, H. Con. Res. 421, 'Recognizing the importance of inheritance rights of women in Africa.' June 18.

Crane, J.L. (2005) 'Map for Gender Reconciliation,' in 'Empowering Women and Men to Use their Gifts Together in Advancing the Gospel,' Alvera Mickelson, ed., Lausanne Occasional Paper No. 53, Lausanne Committee for World Evangelization, in *A New Vision, A New Heart, A Renewed Call*, David Claydon, ed., Volume Two, Pasadena, CA: William Carey Library, 2005. The Map in entirety can be ordered through www.gendermap.org.

Crane, J.L. (2008) 'Innovative Solutions for Greater Justice in Women's Land Rights in Sub-Saharan Africa.' Master's Thesis. School of Peace Studies, University of San Diego.

Division for the Advancement of Women, United Nations (2001)

'Widowhood: invisible women, secluded or excluded,' *Women2000*, December.

Dixon, R. 'Uganda widow wins compensation after fight,' *Los Angeles Times*, 29 April 2013.

Dutt, V. (2010) *Invisible Forgotten Sufferers, The Plight of Widows Around the World, Why the UN Should Recognize International Widows Day, A Research Study commissioned by the Loomba Foundation and presented to the United Nations on International Widows Day, 23 June 2010, Research by Risto F. Harma*. New Delhi: Konark Publishers Pvt Ltd.

Edemikpong, H. (2005) 'Widowhood rites: Nigeria Women's Collective Fights A Dehumanizing Tradition.' *Off Our Backs*. March/April, Vol 35, Issue ¾, 34-35.

Ewelukwa, U.U. (2002) 'Post-colonialism, gender, customary injustice: Widows in African societies.' *Human Rights Quarterly*. May, Vol 24, Issue 2, 424-486.

Fasoranti, O.O. & Aruna, J.O. (2012) 'A Cross-Cultural Comparison of Practices Relating to Widowhood and Widow-Inheritance Among the Igbo and Yoruba in Nigeria,' *Journal of World Anthropology*, Occasional Papers: Volume III, Number 1, 2012.

George, T.O. (2012) 'Policy Response to Widowhood Rites among the Awori of Ogun State, Nigeria,' *American International Journal of Contemporary Research*, Vol. 2, No. 5, May, 188.

Human Rights Watch, "Discrimination in Property and Inheritance Rights and HIV/AIDS," http://www.hrw.org/reports/2003/africa1203/5.htm, accessed 11/9/2012.

IFAD, International Fund for Agricultural Development, United Nations, "Uganda, Ghana and Cote d'Ivoire – The Situation of Widows," http://www.ifad.org/gender/learning/challenges/widows/55.htm, accessed 3 August 2013.

Immigration and Refugee Board of Canada (2002) 'Ashanti widow rituals, steps required, whether the widow can refuse to participate, whether she would be required to marry her husband's relative, and consequences for refusal' [GHA38600.E]. 07 May, http://www.ecoi.net/local_link/176988/293909_de.html.

International Justice Mission (2010), 'Casework Bulletin, 13 April 2010.' http://www.ijm.org/articles/caseworkbulletin.

IRIN PlusNews, 'Kenya: Protecting Widows from Dangerous Customs' http://www.plusnews.org/PrintReport.aspx?ReportId=72821.

Iyer, P. (2005) 'Namibia considers new bill to protect widows and children.' *New York Amsterdam News*. July 21, Vol 96, Issue 30, 2.

Izumi, K. (2007) 'Gender-based violence and property grabbing in Africa: a denial of women's liberty and security.' *Gender and Development*. March, Vol 15, Issue 1, 11-23.

Kabonde, M.P. (1996) 'Widowhood in Zambia: The Effects of Ritual' in *Groaning in Faith: African Women in the Household of God.* Kanyoro, M. & Njoroge, N.J., eds. Nairobi: Acton Publishers, 195-203.

Kanyoro, M. & Njoroge, N.J., eds. (1996) *Groaning in Faith: African Women in the Household of God.* Nairobi: Acton Publishers.

Kirwen, M.C. (1979) *African Widows: An empirical study of the problems of adapting Western Christian teachings on marriage to the leviratic custom for the care of rural widows in four African societies.* Maryknoll: Orbis Books.

Lusaka Times (2011). 'Toothless law under review to curb rising cases of property grabbing.' 21 May, http://www.lusakatimes.com/2011/05/21/toothless-law-review-curb-rising-cases-property-grabbing/, accessed 19 August 2013.

Makatu, M.S. & Wagner, C. & Ruane, I. & Van Schalkwyk, G.J. (2008) 'Discourse analysis of the perceptions of bereavement and bereavement rituals of Tshivenda speaking women.' *Journal of Psychology in Africa.* Vol 18, Issue 4, 573-580.

Mbugua, J. (1994) *Our Time Has Come: African Christian Women Address the Issues of Today.* Grand Rapids: Baker Book House.

Mensah, L. (2013) 'Ghana's extravagant funerals drive families into debt.' World News, 12 June 2013, http://www.upi.com/Top_News/World-News/2013/06/12/Ghanas-extravagant-funerals-drive-families-into-debt/PC-9771371075364/. Accessed 13 September 2013.

Modern Ghana News, (2010) 'Widowhood Rites Still Rife in Northern Regions.' September 30. http://ww.modernghana.com/news/298544/1/widowhood-rites-still-rife-in-northern-regions.html.

Moon, B.K. (2011). Secretary General's Message for 2011, International Widow' Day, June 23. http://www.un.org/en/events/widowsday/2011/sgmessage.shtml, accessed 15 September 2013.

Mutongi, K. (2007) *Worries of the Heart: Widows, Family, and Community in Kenya.* University of Chicago Press.

New African Magazine (2012). 'Empowering Widows through Education,' May, 49.

New York Times (2005) 'AIDS Now Compels Africa to Challenge Widows' 'Cleansing.' May 11, Vol 154, Issue 53211, A1-8.

New York Times Editorial (2004) 'Africa's Homeless Widows.' June 16, Vol 153, Issue 52882, A20.

Nwachuku, D.N. (1992) 'The Christian Widow in African Culture' in T*he Will to Arise: Women, Tradition, and the Church in Africa.* Oduyoye, M.A. & Kanyoro, M.R.A., eds. Eugene: Wipf & Stock Publishers, 54-73.

Nwadinobi, E. *Widowhood: Facts, Feelings and the Law*, a publication of the Widows Development Organisation with the support of the Sigrid Rausing Trust, UK. Enugu, Nigeria. For more information, go to www.widoafrica.org.

Oche, M. (2012) 'Nigeria: Life after our husbands' death is terrible, widows cry out,' *All Africa*. 24 June, http://allafrica.com/stories/printable/201206250277.html.

Odimmegwa, A.O. (2010) 'Widowhood and the Dignity of Womanhood in Igboland: A Pastoral Challenge to the Discipleship of the Roman Catholic Church in Igboland.' Ph.D. Dissertation, Fordham University, New York.

Oduyoye, M.A. & Kanyoro, M.R.A., eds. (1992) *The Will to Arise: Women, Tradition, and the Church in Africa*. Eugene: Wipf & Stock Publishers.

Oketta, K. 'Principles and Practices of Customary Tenure in Acholiland.' Ken Oketta, Ker Kwaro Acholi, PO Box 54, Gulu, Uganda.

Okoye, I. (2000) *The Trial and Other Stories*, African Heritage Press.

Okoye, P.U. (1995) *Widowhood: A Natural or Cultural Tragedy*. Enugu: Nucik Publishers.

Onuh, Emmanuel, "Widows in the Church: Any Protection and Help?" in *Widowhood in the Church and Society*, ed. Aloysius C. Obiwulu (Enugu, Nigeria: Delta Publications Nigeria Ltd., 2009), 94, as reported in Odimmegwa, *op cit*, 107.

Owen, M. (1996) *A World of Widows*. London and New Jersey: Zed Books Ltd.

Peterman, Amber. 'Widowhood and Asset Inheritance in Sub-Saharan Africa: Empirical Evidence from Fifteen Countries.' *Development Policy Review*. Vol. 30, 2012, 543-57.

Potash, B., ed. (1986) *Widows in African Societies, Choices and Constraints*. Stanford: Stanford University Press.

Razavi, S., ed. (2003) *Agrarian Change, Gender and Land Rights*. United Nations Research Institute for Social Development. Oxford: Blackwell Publishing.

Robson, A. (2009) 'Male cleansers for hire.' *New Internationalist*. April, Issue 421, 10.

Rosenblatt, P.C. & Nokosi, B.W. (2007) 'South African Zulu Widows in a Time of Poverty and Social Change.' *Death Studies*. January, Vol 31, Issue 1, 67-85.

Shisanya, Constance R.A. (1996). 'Death Rituals: The Case of the Abaluhya of Western Kenya,' in *Groaning in Faith: African Women in the Household of God*, Kanyoro, Musimbi R.A. and Njoroge, Nyambura, eds. Nairobi: Acton Publishers, 187, 193.

Sinyangwe, B. (2000) *A Cowrie of Hope*. Oxford: Heinemann Educational Publishers.

Somhlaba, N.Z. & Wait, J.W. (2009) 'Stress, Coping Styles and Spousal Bereavement: Exploring Patterns of Grieving Among Black Widowed Spouses in Rural South Africa.' *Journal of Loss and*

Trauma. May/June, Vol 14, Issues 3, 196-210.

South African Government (Pretoria). (2013) 'South Africa: National Widows Forum Launched in Polokwane.' 26 July 2013, http://allafrica.com/stories/201307270110.html, accessed 9 August 2013.

Survivors Fund, Supporting Survivors of the Rwanda Genocide, http://survivors-fund.org.uk/resources/rwandan-history/statistics/. Accessed 3 August 2013.

Uganda Bureau of Statistics, Uganda National Household Survey Findings 2009/2010, http://www.ubos.org/UNHS9010/chapter 11_widows.html, accessed 3 August 2013.

United Nations, IFAD, International Fund for Agricultural Development, 'Uganda, Ghana and Cote d'Ivoire – The Situation of Widows,' http://www.ifad.org/gender/learning/challenges/widows/55.htm, accessed 3 August 2013.

United Nations, 'International Widows Day, Background Information.' http://www.un.org/en/events/widowsday/background.shtml.

United Nations (2001) 'Widowhood: invisible women, secluded or excluded,' *Women2000*, Division for the Advancement of Women, December.

Von Struensee, Vanessa, JD, MPH (2004) 'Widows, Aids, Health and Human Rights in Africa.'

Wanyeki, L.M., ed. (2003) *Women and Land in Africa, Culture, Religion and Realizing Women's Rights.* London/New York: Zed Books Ltd. Cape Town: David Philip Publishers.

Widows for Peace through Democracy, Speech by Margaret Owen, http://www.widowsforpeace.org/, accessed 29 September 2013.

Widows Rights International (2012) '2012 International Widow's Day: Will the widow's plight be over?' No. 20, August.

Widows Rights International (2008) 'Women's Inheritance Rights to Land and Housing.' Womens Land Link Africa, http://www.widowsrights.org/landlink.html. Accessed 5/2/08.

WUNRN, Global Action on Widowhood and Widows for Peace through Democracy, 'Include Marital Status and Widowhood in the MDGs, Essential Yet Overlooked Component for Achieving the MDGs by 2015.' http://www.wunrn.com/news/2010/07_10/07_12_10/071210_mdgs.htm

WEBSITES

ADOPT A WIDOW: www.adoptawidow.org
HOPE INTERNATIONAL: www.hopeinternational.org
INTERNATIONAL JUSTICE MISSION: www.ijm.org
TIRZAH INTERNATIONAL: www.tirzah.org
YOUTH WITH A MISSION RWANDA: www.ywamrwanda.com

WITH SPECIAL THANKS TO...

My father, who instilled a sense of justice in me from a young age. My mother, who treated blacks with dignity, unlike the culture of the Deep South where we lived. Chris Crane, who understands my heart for Africa and need to fulfill my God-given destiny. Andrew Crane, my first book reader/brainstormer.

Sandi and Scott Tompkins, editors *extraordinaire.*

Friends, colleagues, and African hosts:

Evelyn Wills, Janet Lambert, Pam Strickler, WOW, Deanna Austin, Oona Noon, Ory Tamsen, Tom Allen, Betty Shimozono, Mark Slomka, David Hamilton, Robin and James Balch, Lauren Hasson and Lifestreams, Audra Baumgarth, Bodie and Brock Thoene, Kim Schuette, Gary Bretow, Jim Murphy, Renee DiToro, Reuben Thiessen, Yvonne and Tim Brown, Cheryl Miller, Mark Griffo II, Mark Woods, Lee Ann Otto, the Peace Possee, Lisa Newmeyer, Emily Onyango, Peace Nihorimbere, Emily Voorhies, John Crews, Esme Bowers, Robyn and David Claydon, the Lausanne Movement, Dean and Carolyn Taylor, Chris Gander, Kwabena Darkoh, Katie Nienow, Dale Hanson Burke, Maureen Menard, Deborah Oyella, Evelyn Bagson, Mary and Method Kamanzi, Raphaelle De Marliave Armstrong, Robert Briggs, Gary Veurink, Mimi Haddad, Jane Overstreet, Allah Asri, La Jolla Community Church, Dionne Archibeck, Lauren Galloway, Lorraine Poer, the Rwanda Association of University Women, Julia Cameron, Alida Lopez, Hipolito Zamorra, Hope International, International Justice Mission, Sinapi Aba Trust, Tirzah International, Youth With A Mission Rwanda.

And all the widows and others across Africa who shared their stories and insights with me.

ABOUT THE AUTHOR

Jane Leonard Crane was born in Augusta, Georgia, the Deep South of the United States, and raised in the tender care of African-American maids and babysitters. From a young age, she was grieved by the treatment of blacks in her hometown and deeply affected by that injustice. Her first "book," at age six, was about an African-American woman.

Through her graduate work on women's land issues in Sub-Saharan Africa, Crane discovered the desperate situation of widows in that region. But the topic had been largely ignored. So she spent four years traveling to Africa and doing academic research to document the plight of widows there. What she found was so dire she began Adopt A Widow, similar to a sponsored-child program but for the benefit of African widows (adoptawidow.org). For this, she uses her experience on the boards of multiple nonprofit organizations.

Given Africa's strong religious focus, Crane draws on her own faith and advocacy for women internationally. She authored the "Map for Gender Reconciliation," examining biblical passages about women, and has taught on it in multiple nations. She contributed on the topic of women to the "Cape Town Commitment" produced by the world's most representative gathering of Christians to date (the Lausanne Movement's Third World Congress, 2010). In 2003, she opened in prayer for Billy Graham in front of 46,000 people in her hometown stadium.

Crane holds a Master's in Peace and Justice from the University of San Diego School of Peace Studies, and makes her home in San Diego, California, USA. She travels to Africa on a regular basis.

CPSIA information can be obtained at www.ICGtesting.com
Printed in the USA
BVOW03s1606090514

352541BV00001B/1/P